Red Letter Words

by Shakespeare, Marlowe, Beckett &

A Gentleman of Cambridge

Robert Pennant Jones

and his granddaughters
Lily and Alana McGeough

Riches from a Theatrical Life

First published in Great Britain in 2024 by The Seven Stars Project.

Copyright © Robert Pennant Jones 2024.

Robert Pennant Jones has asserted his right under the Copyright, Designs and Patents Act 1988 to be identified as the author of this work.

Edited, designed and produced by Tandem Publishing
http://tandempublishing.yolasite.com

ISBN: 978-1-3999-9637-2

10 9 8 7 6 5 4 3 2 1

A CIP catalogue record for this book is available from the British Library.

Printed and bound in Great Britain by CPI Group (UK) Ltd, Croydon CR0 4YY.

The endpapers are of *The Poet and the Painter*, a picture by Ronnie Copas (1997).

For Sheila
With love and admiration
For over sixty years of life together

The text has three sorts of reference marks:

1. QR Code references, e.g. [QR1]. These identify performed extracts that can be accessed via your smartphone through the relevant QR codes on pages 210–212, with timings. They are identified as:
A: audio
V: video (some via YouTube)
N: picture and audio note

2. References to those Red Letter quotations not already identified in the text, e.g. [1]. They are listed on pages 207–209.

3. References to photographs and illustrations in the plate section, e.g. [P1].

https://www.redletterwords.co.uk/

Contents

FOREWORD

I have chosen to call this book *Red Letter Words*, prompted by a piece of dialogue in *Hamlet*:

> What do you read my Lord?
> Words Words Words…
> The satirical rogue says here that old men have grey beards … and that they have a plentiful lack of wit.

Well, at time of writing, my beard is white – I think it is white Sir, [(1)] – and I hope I have not completely lost my wit.

I frequently drop a few names of note and show off by quoting a range of poetic gems, to enhance, however frailly, the reputations of notable poetic masters.

My family politely endures these performances; friends tolerate these indulgences; more distant acquaintances may admire them momentarily; but they tend to forget, as soon as done. [(2)]

And now I reflect that the quotations, the words, are the stars of my subsequent efforts, and justify a book to inspire my grand-daughters, and should therefore stand out in the text, for which the colour red is the obvious tinct. "Why red letter?" asked one of them. I explained how the medieval church calendars of Saints' Days picked out the important ones in red. Confronted with an iniquitous contract, Lord Denning in the Court of Appeal once suggested a 'Red Hand Test': "Some clauses which I have seen would need to be printed in red ink on the face of the document with a red hand pointing to it before the notice could be held to be sufficient."

I achieved a 2:2 degree in English at Cambridge and spent much time in undergraduate theatre productions. Many of the quotations in this book were learned at that time.

One of the things I learned early in my theatrical efforts at university was that these were never good enough to make a career in the theatre worthwhile. My decision to be accepted and enter a thirty-five-year career in the international oil business brought rich rewards to myself and my family, for which I remain entirely grateful.

I must acknowledge that the financial security I enjoyed during my career with BP, and now with a generous pension, has enabled me to maintain a standard of life and enjoy its varied interests far more than I could have managed from the stage.

I would add that my degree made my parents very proud and was a dividend for the sacrifices they had made in providing me with a suitable education to get me to Cambridge. It remains that I am the only member of their family to have achieved this to date.

And my own family, brought up with all this, has been and remains a huge source of joy to me and Sheila, my wife of sixty years, which somehow endorses there being some value in these particular achievements.

I have ordered the book in three sections, the first being auto-biographical, with accounts of my education, business life and involvement in the theatre. My business career gave me the means to be able to pursue a retirement career in artistic projects, mainly based on my work in the theatre.

The second section contains accounts of several of these projects that have occupied me over the years, some of which I have previously printed for the record, these being the more successful ones.

The third section consists of more general artistic precepts, including short red-letter references to other writers who have inspired me, and some other suggestions to develop artistic ideas that might be of interest.

And it's the red letter words that I particularly recommend to the reader. Read them over and over, maybe aloud; I find hearing them for oneself adds to their merit and worth. Further acquaintance with them will give a lifetime's pleasure and satisfaction.

As well as highlighting the quotations in this way, I have added additional references, namely QR codes, to some passages of the book whereby the reader can experience recorded material on my website and elsewhere, to illustrate the text further.

Archie Rice
The Entertainer

APOLOGY, AUDIENCE, FAME

Getting Known

Apology

Of making many books there is no end. [3]

For most existing books, their relevance and readers are gone. For some there is a lingering relevance beyond their time. For a few, their interest and entertainment retain their readership. And there are immortal classics for which we thank God, if we believe God and the afterlife exist.

So what is the point of writing another book if I believe that my life and experiences are ultimately of little interest to anyone but myself?

Well, I feel there is something from my experiences worth recording and, maybe, influencing a small audience. I shall not need it as testimony of my worth at heaven's gate. But it may give a few insights that are valuable to others. And these precepts are those that I have gained, sometimes from books. So the outcome of my recording them in yet another book should be to prolong their work for a few years after my death. But deep down I reflect, with an inward sigh, that all is vanity, and little justification for yet another book.

Audience

You've been a good audience … very good. A very *good* audience. Let me know where you're working tomorrow night – and I'll come and see you. [4]

We all need an audience, and as an actor I perhaps more so than most. Writing this book prompts the question: who is it for? It may be my two granddaughters Lily and Alana, and, maybe, a few others, especially if they become involved in the arts, particularly theatre.

There is a special bond between grandfathers and grandchildren. My own grandfathers were Myddleton Pennant Jones (Granddad), father to my father Glyn Maredudd Pennant Jones and Percy Thomas Robert Gillett (P.T.R.), father to my mother Mary. Granddad contributed significantly to my education, as I have done for my grandchildren. P.T.R. taught me a love of books and pictures and both Lily and Alana, my daughter Helena and Declan's children, have a keen artistic eye. I have recently sold part of P.T.R.'s book collection to fund a vehicle for Lily and Alana's artistic enterprises in the future.

There seems to be some value in skipping generations in these relationships. This is not to diminish the importance of the bonds between parents and their children, of course, far from it, but to recognise this extra relationship as particularly beneficial. As I have benefited from my grandfathers' part in my own life so I hope Lily and Alana, the main audience for this book, will profit from my experiences. And the thought that their grandchildren may one day derive some benefit too from their great great, and even great great great great grandparent is a seductive one and reason enough to write.

As Lily found at an early age, one of my personal vanities is my ability to quote considerable passages from the great authors, which I do to show off, but also to induce an admiration for that author in my audience. I persuade myself that my motive for quoting is more of the latter rather than the former. The authors I mainly quote are Shakespeare, Marlowe and Beckett, the reputations of none of them actually needing much of a boost from me. But I would like to offer my granddaughters a selection of these for their delight. Indeed at the Millennium, when they were still infants, I took out an advertisement in the *International Herald Tribune* (now sadly subsumed by the *New York Times*) giving them five special quotations for their future lives. The five were intended to give them an idea of the importance I attach to the artistic life. They appear in 'Some Quotations for Life'.

While accepting that the main audience for this book may be Lily and Alana, there may be an audience for some insights gained from over forty years of writing a diary which concentrates largely on my artistic life. To read the diaries would be too much to ask of anyone, even for me to reread them. So, what comes is partly an editing of what is already recorded, partly a reminiscence and partly a comment based on contemporary experience by which we old men judge the past and, less and less, plan for the future. *Getting Known,* [5] if that happens, is likely to be slow. So not for fame one writes. The effort of writing is for personal satisfaction.

Fame

... she comes unlooked for, if she comes at all... [6]

My son Owen asked me when he was seventeen (so I was in my mid forties) how I had come to terms with not having achieved any sort of fame. I probably muttered that there may be time for that, but doubting it in my heart, I would almost certainly have quoted Gray.

> Full many a flower is born to blush unseen,
> And waste its beauty on the desert air. [7]

Incidentally, my friend Michael Burrell, the actor and a Gray scholar among his other talents, the day before he died corrected me: "It's *sweetness*" he said, "not *beauty*"; never mind, when the idea is right one can surely forgive my gift for misquotation.

I have spent much time trying to track down the identity of the anonymous author of an eighteenth-century pamphlet called *The Lady's Preceptor*, which I admire for the quality of its writing and for its gentle urbanity. The author wrote under the pseudonym "A Gentleman of Cambridge", and made only the slightest attempt (when he was near to death) to hint at his identity to the world. Any fame I might achieve for him by correctly unveiling his identity as the author of *The Lady's Preceptor* would be unlikely to make much difference to his shade looking down on my efforts.

And do the shades look down? What would be the point? To congratulate our own shades when they finally meet up that their fame had been ratcheted up a bit? To have something to chat about in heaven as a distraction from the eternal harpist? One might like to think so, but without much confidence I suggest.

A few will attain Fame – not the transitory fame of celebrity – but Fame that lasts for generations. Owen's question came when I was the Chief Executive of BP in Malaysia, briefly famous I suppose… But that was in another country, [8] fleeting fame with a limited audience. And with my range of literary props – quotations from the masters – and genuinely despising the transitory fame of modern celebrity, it was easy enough to answer Owen, particularly if one is not famous.

And if one is famous in this life, consider Samuel Beckett, for example, whose biography by James Knowlson was entitled *Damned to Fame* and showed how well-wishers and hangers-on (like me) interfered not only with his work but with his personal life too. His courtesy and diligence in satisfying the claims of others became a burden to him. This, incidentally, is one of the arguments I adduce for wondering if there is an afterlife where one can mingle with one's heroes. Think of the queues in heaven waiting for chats with Shakespeare for example, or Mozart, or Botticelli. And what's in it for them but a surfeit of recognition. Fame on earth is overwhelmingly transitory. Ian McKellen, on the red carpet at a film premiere, told me of being mobbed by hundreds of fans, many of them children, ruefully explaining "It's Gandalf that they love, not me."

Poetic fame has been likened to the echo caused by a falling feather reaching the bottom of the Grand Canyon. I used to be encouraged by a similar image: that the environmental impact of the Trans-Alaska Pipeline on the State of Alaska was the same as that of a silk thread laid on the Island of Manhattan. The fame of an actor like Colley Cibber was described by him as faint echoes in the minds of those surviving members of the audience who happened to see a particular performance. These days, of course, performances can be remembered, with millions of images being created each day of such performances, and of much else that is negligible. Even if the inclination exists, so much time must be expended by so many to see the record of such performances, that only a few will even be seen let alone remain or become famous. Cibber wrote an autobiography – much of his fame today rests on the written memoir. Shakespeare too recognised that the writer's reputation outlasts all other claims for immortal fame.

So, writing my own conclusions about what is, has been, important to me is essentially for myself. Do Lily and Alana really want or need these thoughts; or would they not rather make up their minds for themselves? Of course they would.

And yet I am still minded to write even so late in my life and see where it leads.

The procrastination may finally be over.

Perhaps the best is simply to carry on, leaving fame to fate, should the fates perchance allow that. [9]

Creon, Antigone, Oedipus
Oedipus at Colonus

EDUCATION

Willingly to School

I had a privileged education. My parents made sacrifices to send me to prep schools, a public school, Bradfield College, assisted in part by my grandfather and a generous county council, offset by the (low) value of Exhibitions I gained, and helped by some judicious gains on the stock exchange.

The privilege goes beyond money. Some excellent teachers accounted for much of that privilege. H. J. O. Marshall (I never knew what the initials stood for) was headmaster of my second prep school. All I really remember of him was, as senior classics master, he insisted on us eleven- to twelve-year-olds learning Latin grammar before lessons each day, even at the expense of cutting short tennis-ball football in the yard. I can still recite today all the Latin prepositions that take the different tenses, either when "state not motion" or the reverse applies.

At Bradfield my housemaster was Arthur Sopwith, a distinguished mathematician, whose moral precepts, austere yet benevolent, inform me still. He also advised me, when I was top of the advanced maths stream, that I had reached my intellectual ceiling in that subject and, since I was about to embark on preparing for university, would be well advised to do so in English rather than try to keep up with slower but more gifted mathematicians at university.

These English studies were nurtured by Leslie Wilson and David Raeburn. Wilson, a splendidly Falstaffian figure, but with a far sounder moral compass, was a great Shakespearean. And I had the considerable help of a school book, *An English Sampler*, edited by (I think) a distant relative of my housemaster – S. S. Sopwith, a master at Shrewsbury.

Leslie Wilson prepared me for Cambridge. David Raeburn, a distinguished classicist, was a new member of staff brought in to direct the Greek play at Bradfield, performed every three years.

I should also mention Colonel J. D. Hills MC MA (Magister Imperator as he used to inscribe School Prizes), an ex-second-master at Eton, who used to wear gown and mortar board atop a white shirted wing collar and white bow tie. He quoted a number of lines which I still remember:

> Who is Silvia? What is she,
> That all our swains commend her?
> Holy, fair and wise is she... [10]

and he added his own comment: In that order, gentlemen, if you please.

And it was not only the classics he quoted, as this exchange in his study before a class of new bright young things:

Hills: Come in, come in, come in gentlemen. Sit down, sit down, sit down. You are?
Boy: Lower History 4, Sir.
Hills: No, No! Sit down, sit down, sit down. You're rocking the boat!

I had an interview for a place at Cambridge because I showed promise, as I learned, in my English paper, despite having little time to prepare having abandoned my Maths/Physics/Chemistry specialisms after A levels. I chose St Catharine's College simply because they, and Selwyn, held a joint entrance paper and interviewed the latest in the year of all the colleges at Cambridge.

My interviewer was a W. B. Yeats scholar, Brigadier Tom Henn, who asked me two questions which, I believe, gained me my place, and indeed my entrance Exhibition.

The two questions were to ask why I had chosen James Shirley to quote in my paper. "Who?" I said. He showed me my hand-written quotation –

> The glories of our blood and state
> Are shadows, not substantial things; [11]

And I quoted the rest of it from memory, a passage in *An English Sampler* I liked. James Shirley, I was told, was the most distinguished literary author of the college. The second question involved asking me to perform Cassius, which I was due to play later in the summer. "But I haven't learned it yet" I said, offering instead a short passage from Antigone's threnody in the Greek play I had performed in Greek, the previous summer. Much later I learned that Ian McKellen, with whom I was to do tutorials, had performed Once more unto the breach [12] as his qualification for an entrance Exhibition, which Tom Henn awarded both of us.

I came across the word Exhibitioner in *The Times*, listing the Scholarships and Exhibitions awarded at schools and universities. It occurred to me that my career has been that of an Exhibitioner: good enough to be taken notice of, but below top class. In my case (and Ian McKellen's) my Exhibition at St Catharine's was withdrawn when I achieved only a 2:2 in Part I. Tom Henn, who had awarded it on the promise shown in the entrance exam and at interview, added by way of consolation as he informed me of the decision, "But you can always refer to yourself as an Open Entrance Exhibitioner of this College". As I was also an Exhibitioner at Bradfield (£30 per year), the word is not inappropriate. Both in business and in retirement I have made my mark, if not an exhibition of myself.

I had to do National Service and did this before going up to Cambridge, giving myself more time to catch up with essential preparatory reading. My National Service was in the Royal Air Force – 5011097 Pilot Officer Pennant Jones served in Northern Ireland (RAF Langford Lodge) and Wales (RAF Pembroke Dock).

So, a privileged education, which I have benefited from and which encouraged my natural abilities to be relevant to my life. And, as I said to my grandchildren as they embarked on their university careers, further education is about learning how to learn; not necessarily what is learned at university.

Cassius
Julius Caesar

Shylock
The Poet and the Painter
(Notice the *Financial Times* in Shylock's hand)

BUSINESS

My pleasure, business [13]

Earning a living is a major preoccupation of us all between the ages of twenty and sixty, second only to family in most cases. Here am I, retired (for nearly thirty years), supported by a lovely family for whom I provided, secure with a pension that pays for my retirement which I choose to spend "faffing around at the fringes of the theatre".

As to my business life, I had thought of subtitling this book with the question 'What is the value of an arts degree?', and not a brilliant one in my case. This chapter, maybe, provides an answer.

I was lucky to be employed by BP for my entire working life. My career in BP was indeed a fortunate one. In an expansionist era for the company, my particular age group (e.g. pre–war babies) were always ahead of the curve in being offered, and accepting, new and exciting roles in that expansion; provided you were good enough, of course. In my case I (and my family) were lucky enough to enjoy two-plus years' postings to Germany, the USA, Sweden and Malaysia. These postings and subsequent regional involvements, usually requiring travel, gave me a deep knowledge of the three main continents I was involved with: Europe, North America and Asia, notably the Far East. All these gave me an international outlook on business and life.

Today, lifetime employment in one company is a rarity as the pyramid of managerial command, which in my day followed that of the armed forces, one manager commanding three or four, became later in my career one to ten or twelve, making heightened competition for those increasingly rare management positions. Again, I was lucky enough, or valuable enough to my peers, to manage in my forties and fifties and to retire when I was ready.

One of the options for those being made redundant was to go into business for oneself. I do not have experience of working for myself but I have observed that this is fraught with potential disaster. My advice to entrepreneurs starting up consists of the mundane, yet vital, points that need to be addressed:

> What is the relationship between the capital put into the business and the revenue to be earned?
>
> Have an accountant/finance director you can trust.
>
> Cash flow is paramount.
>
> How much are you going to depend on others (cost); and how much are you going to invest in your own labour?
>
> What 'edge' does your business have over others, and is it easily copyable?
>
> How much of your budget is based on hope rather than realism?

Talking of hope brings me to my particular contributions made to BP – some of which may be applicable to anyone in business, whether working for someone else or for oneself.

I begin by quoting Charles Revson, the founder of Revlon,

> In the factory I make cosmetics; in the store I sell hope.

This illustrates the fundamental difference between marketing and selling. I was a marketer in BP, which involved thinking about gasoline retailing. Gasoline is sold at petrol stations, but competition meant having to accept lower and lower margins which raised the question as to whether we should do more at petrol stations to remunerate the capital involved in the facilities and in the site itself. In my day the emergence of convenience stores at petrol stations was the main example of finding an answer to the question, and BP, aided by me and others, contributed to that change. So, the difference between marketing and selling was indeed fundamental to the development of retail business at petrol stations, encapsulated by this definition:

> Selling is getting rid of what you've got
> (i.e. petrol in this case)
>
> Marketing is having what you can get rid of
> (i.e. "convenience" groceries)

The businessman dismisses this as mere sophistry at his peril.

The basic point is brilliantly underlined by the task I used to set young aspiring marketers with this problem:

> You read in a trade magazine that, last year, the ABC company sold 250,000 ¼ inch drill bits. What is a marketer's interpretation of that piece of information?
>
> Step 1   Silence.
>
> Step 2   I announce a prize of £10, extracted from my wallet and put on the table, for the first correct answer.
>
> Step 3   Each shot at an answer to cost £1 to be added to the prize.
>
> Step 4   30 various wrong ideas about last year's figures, year to date, research, competitor reactions

etc. bringing prize pot to around £40.

Step 5   The shyest member of the audience mumbles
the right answer and takes the prize.

Yes, it takes that long. The answer? A marketer's interpretation of
the trade magazine's clipping is:

> Last year, at least 250,000 ¼ inch HOLES were
> needed. Holes – no one is in the slightest bit interested
> in buying ¼ inch drill bits unless one perceives the
> need for a HOLE of that size.

And when it comes to advertising your wares it's the same
principle, for example:

> Sell the sizzle, not the steak.

Much later in my career I included advertising in my portfo-
lio, when I was concerned with BP's reputation in the outside
world. One of the misconceptions of the day, rather like misconceptions between selling and marketing – they are the same
thing aren't they? – is that of the difference between identity and
image. Misconceived advertisers used to think that image can be
created by the brilliance of their advertising. Not so. Image is
the cumulation of impressions that the outside world has about
the company. Advertising is a tiny part of that, and, often, mis-
directed advertising far from enhancing a company's image can
detract from it. Image is not in our power. But it is in one's power
to set about creating an identity, which is the way a company does
business, not the least through the quality of one's productions,
their value for money and a whole range of perceived qualities of
one's employees – the ways we do business.

I had over six years in Government and Public Affairs (GPA) and Corporate Communications (CCM) in BP, heading up the latter as my last job in the company. In defending the money invested by the company in CCM from colleagues looking for cuts, in what is often perceived as not contributing to profit, I used my Shakespeare knowledge to quote Iago's:

> Who steals my purse steals trash…
> 'Twas mine, 'tis his, and has been slave to thousands;
> But he that filches from me my good name,
> Robs me of that which not enriches him,
> And makes me poor indeed. [14]

I was lucky enough to leave BP when its reputation was high. The wisdom of Iago's lines was underlined when the Gulf of Mexico tragedy hit BP's reputation, and pocket, so hard that it was feared it might never recover. Better communication may have mitigated some of these losses – BP was treated disgracefully by the Americans, and it was BP who bore most of the blame and financial pain. In recognising the wisdom of Iago in this context it must be noted that he has already undermined it with:

> Reputation is an idle and most false imposition;
> oft got without merit, and lost without deserving… [15]

As to communication itself I also used to quote:

> No man is the lord of anything,
> Though in and of him there be much consisting,
> Till he communicate his parts to others. [16]

In personal terms this means not hiding one's light under a bushel (it was often said in BP that marketing oneself to one's bosses and colleagues was the only real marketing practised by marketers). This is, of course, important in getting on in one's career. And if one's career flourishes into promotions, even to the extent of being promoted above one's qualifications, it is vital to maintain skills in communication: listening, making connections and not delegating to others what one does really well. In my case I was a good editor of material, a good listener and able to connect with a wide variety of colleagues. My retirement speech to the managing directors was to remind them of Cleopatra's treatment of the messenger bringing bad news:

Thou shalt be whipp'd with wire, and stew'd in brine. [17]

I was pleased to retire as the corporate messenger not having suffered such indignities at their hands.

Perhaps the most important quality when working for a corporation, or for another, is that everything one does is geared to the employer's benefit. An employee who is working for the benefit of the employer will refer to the employer as We; if he uses They it is certain that he is putting his own interests first. False expense claims are far more likely from the "They" speaker than the "We" speaker. But it is not just expenses – every action by the employee must be intended for the benefit of the employer.

As a general rule I found the following ideas and actions helpful both for the company and my own career. I am by nature a morning person so it is easy to get in early to work. As I had an important private life with family and with the theatre I used to leave in time to resume my private life in the early evening. Later in my career I was sometimes asked, even required, to stay late for a business meeting. My usual response if this clashed with an important date such as a family engagement or a theatre rehearsal or performance was to offer alternative dates if possible. This way only a few clashes materialised. Having one diary for all engagements made such diary management possible. Offering breakfast meetings the following day was one solution that often proved effective. Later in my career, for meetings I could not attend and for which my input was desirable, I used to offer and indeed execute a video contribution. Getting meetings with a busy boss was also not always easy, especially if he was pressed for time before embarking on his travels. A solution to that was to accompany him in his car to the airport, returning with the car, business having been concluded.

Getting the detail correct in business is of great importance. One huge error from my early career gives this some context. I was in my first job, responsible for submitting bids to win aviation fuel business around the world against the competition. It happened in the event that we lost business at an airport we had expected to win and I was summoned to my boss to receive a dressing down that threatened my career. I had quoted the price I had been told to submit but, unfortunately, I had expressed this in pence per imperial gallon rather than in US cents per US gallon, numbers which, at the time, were in fact nearly the same. The error meant that the price I submitted was not successful. I left the office with my tail between my legs.

A lesson from this is to be clear about detail, and this goes as well to other professional qualities such as getting people's names right and correctly spelled with correct titles in any correspondence, which itself must always be grammatically correct and properly punctuated.

One of my earlier bosses had a clever tactic for winning business such as airline fuel contracts. Much of the negotiation of such contracts took place in the pub, and the story goes that he used to visit the pub in question beforehand to prepare for the subsequent drinking encounter. He would introduce himself to the barman with the question "Would you be able to recognise me when I order drinks later?" The answer "yes" was not difficult for the barman since he was of stocky build with a florid face, a white moustache, a carnation in his button hole and a monocle. On receiving this assent, he instructed the barman to fill an empty vodka bottle with water and put it in a special place behind the bar. He then said that when ordering drinks for the group he would add "And the usual for me" which was to be a double vodka on the rocks. Each time the barman pocketed the price of the double vodka for himself. The result was that whereas the airline negotiators got increasingly jolly, our man was stone cold sober. It was said that many a contract was secured in this way. And, of course, he eventually claimed full expenses for the drinks.

And on expenses my son Owen and I have long derived pleasure from these red letter words (which we choose slightly to misquote) from Beckett's *All That Fall*:

> We have saved fivepence.
> We could have saved sixpence;
> But at what cost?

The point being that there is often more than a monetary value to commercial transactions.

My most charismatic boss was David Simon, who was appointed CEO of BP when Bob Horton was ousted. On his promotion he set about drafting a mission statement to return the company to its former glory. He showed me his idea: Performance, Reputation, Teamwork … or PRT for short. I wondered if we might not alter the order to TPR in that Teamwork will lead to Performance and restore Reputation but he stuck with PRT, later praising my contribution to its success though my idea had been ignored. This illustrates two points I have been making – we were both working for the same side and exactness of language is important. And my suggestion was intended to enhance David's new role. And, incidentally, the words Performance, Reputation and Teamwork apply equally to a successful theatre company.

One of my contemporaries at Cambridge, who wanted eventually to gain international experience, had also joined the oil industry on graduating and was accepted by Shell Mex and BP, at that time the UK's marketing company run by Shell (with a 60 per cent interest) on behalf of BP (40 per cent).

Joining a totally UK company, my contemporary had backed the wrong horse while I, who had joined BP for a possible career in marketing, became liable for overseas postings to learn the necessary skills. And how lucky I was in the places where I was sent.

Hamburg was the first city where we went as a family in 1967 – Sheila with Owen, then just over one, with Helena destined to be born there in 1968. We lived in a flat near the Alster (there was a story that instead of raining bombs on the area the RAF pilots dropped leaflets saying "Don't worry, we are coming there to live when the war is over"). I observed much of German bureaucratic methodology with a mixture of approval and doubt. The formality and discipline for hard work were admirable, but the unquestioning adherence to given routines not so. There are two examples. One: capital investment at service stations. The given rule was that once the petrol throughput reached a given total, a second or third car repair workshop could be added to the site to improve the sales of lubricants. This overlooked the emerging truth that repairing cars at petrol stations was vastly inefficient and unprofitable for the dealer and the provider of capital. Yet, if it was in the company's regulations, the money would be spent. The second concerned the regional distribution manager (responsible for supplying petrol stations via the fleet of road tankers) who demanded a vehicle fleet of sufficient capacity to service peak demand e.g. on the day before Good Friday, rather than having a fleet of a size to keep delivery costs fitting to the year-round demand.

At the time, Germany was still going through post-war deprivations and one of the prized benefits of such a company was the supply of subsidised lunches for staff – the quality of the food being as much prized as the economic benefits – blood sausage was an especial favourite in our Hamburg office. Lunch time was staggered since the dining facilities were too small to cater for all the staff at one time. Our meal time was 1.40 (the last but one sitting) which meant that at 11.20 we were only halfway to lunchtime. A middle-aged colleague used to take a sandwich out of his lunch box at precisely 11.20, muttering "Der Magen muss auch arbeiten" – the stomach has to work too.

One of the advantages of such postings was of course financial, being paid (thanks in part to my earlier work on overseas allowances) rather more than we were perhaps worth. Another, in our case, that we were able to return to London, to our previous accommodation (which had been sublet for the duration) and reacquaint ourselves with life in London and a career in the company at the company's headquarters.

Our next posting, to New York, was probably the most important of our lives. I was asked, on my 32nd birthday, by Christopher Laidlaw, at that time the Deputy Chairman, whether I would accept a post in the USA, ostensibly to check that a new acquisition by the company was being properly handled, but in fact to get better acquainted with the staff of the new organisation. It took about 30 seconds for me to say yes. To the remark that I was essentially a company spy I would not disagree. My role was technically to observe and report on oil products marketing in the USA and report back any interesting new developments to London. This meant quite a lot of travel and I did manage to visit many different states in my two years. I found out that the USA retail scene was in advance of Europe in its pricing policy – competitive prices to maximise "ideal" throughputs at petrol stations. But Europe was well ahead of the US in self service and convenience shopping.

Living in New York (E77th Street at York Avenue) with a young family was exhilarating. Owen had his first primary education at PS158, right opposite our apartment. Helena joined a pre-school playgroup in the John Jay Park. We spent our weekends in our garden – the wonderful Central Park to which we cycled. Owen and I got to appreciate baseball with the world champion New York Mets – we saw Cleon Jones hit a home run at Shea Stadium and watched Tom Seaver pitch. We both enjoyed the TV coverage of the Fischer–Spassky Chess Championship. We visited the City Opera where Norman Treigle in Boito's *Mefistofele* gave one of the most memorable performances I have ever witnessed. I joined an Off Off Broadway theatre group and, when our time was up, mulled over whether an extended stay in America or another return to London was for us. The decision was not in reality close, but the energy of New York and the excitement were pausers in our decision, which came down to education of the children, family at home and a continuing career enhanced by the US experience.

If New York was exciting, Sweden was dull – not the least on account of the long winters. Luckily we were there for three summers and one of the winters was a white winter where snow falls lit up the drab buildings more pleasantly than when there was little actual snow. And the long summer days were lovely, including when we explored Stockholm's archipelago by boat. Professionally I had become more senior and was made responsible for merchandising at petrol stations and refining the network to improve performance or to lose the overheads devoted to marginal stations.

The most important thing in running a petrol station, or any small business, is that there is nothing inherently difficult in getting every detail of the operation right. But what is difficult is getting every detail right at the same time. And, as the old adage has it, the customer is always right.

Helena's first school was the Anglo-American school and Owen began to board at his prep school, joining us for school holidays. We spent a good deal of time at Täby Galopp, the horse racing track on the outskirts of the city.

Our final overseas posting, when I was in my forties, was to BP Malaysia where I was given my first command, to run the company and to achieve a clean break with our regional head-quarters in BP Singapore. I managed this by some judicious staff appointments and, for the last time in my career, managing a company for which I had the necessary knowledge for all parts of its operation, which at the time was to establish a new operations depot, expand the retail network and maintain good relations with the Government, with our BP Exploration colleagues and our regional headquarters.

As a generalisation, in Malaysia Commerce was handled by the Chinese (whose ancestors had been brought in by the British to do the tin mining), the Law was handled by the Indians while the Malays, as a majority, handled the Government. We were told to prefer Malays in appointments, not always easy for lack of suitable qualifications, to improve the general balance of the races in different parts of the economy. As English was the common tongue from its colonial past, I was able to operate successfully in that environment. And with children now at boarding school and the services of Yano our housekeeper and Shueb, a splendid Malay chauffeur, life was very agreeable as well as being financially rewarding. For such expatriates boarding school fees were heavily subsidised by the company which greatly improved our finances and way of life.

BP Malaysia was the last job I held in which I knew as much as any of my staff about the jobs I was responsible for managing. It was with events outside the company that I began to experience the wider responsibilities of management. The "Buy British Last" campaign of the Malaysian Prime Minister, reacting to Mrs Thatcher's treatment of overseas students in British universities, including Malaysian students, needed careful handling with other affected companies, in which I played a role. The issue eventually went away and I gave a presentation to visiting BP colleagues that led to my next position in the Government and Public Relations department, concerned with the reputation of the company with outside bodies. More importantly it meant that my future role in the company was in general management.

Subsequent jobs in London added to my already considerable European experiences, as when I became Assistant Regional Co-ordinator for the United States and later Regional Co-ordinator for East Asia (China, Japan, Taiwan, Hong Kong, Indonesia, Singapore, Malaysia, Philippines and Thailand) at a time when the company was expanding its interests there, not only on the retail side but also in Exploration and Chemicals. My international experiences are thus quite deep in Europe, North America and the Far East to the neglect, maybe, of my own country, though I did head up BP Oil in the UK towards the end of my career.

A few general business precepts seem worth recording:

> Keep a skill that you do better than any of your staff. In my case it was editing and presentation; and listening.

Distrust any member of staff who uses "They" instead of "We" when talking about the company.

Make sure every action you take is for the benefit of the company rather than for self. The three stakeholders in any enterprise need their interests to be kept in balance if each is to flourish. If shareholders take too much in dividends, or customers in prices or employees in salaries, the balance will be broken and

the enterprise will sicken. [18]

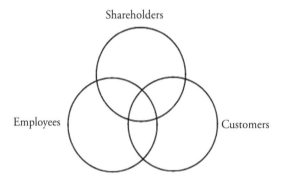

Maintain wide and discreet regular contacts with senior colleagues and junior staff.

Be especially close to those providing services – I have been particularly helped in significant ways by my personal assistants in most of my jobs.

Never stand in the way of anyone's promotion. And plan for one's own successor.

But always be aware of the "Danish Bicycle Race" – where the last over the line after a few circuits is removed from the race, the same happening at the end of each subsequent circuit, leaving two to finish the race between them. In business removing, say, 10 per cent of staff each year, replacing them with new blood, is certain to improve company performance. But be generous with what faces the 10 per cent.

Get to meetings before everyone else to secure the seat most favourable for the body politics of the day. The impression given will be that it is somehow "your" meeting.

Never be late.

Regularly chat with staff on a one-to-one basis – regular "doctor's rounds", i.e. visiting their place of work, reveals much about performance and trust.

Though not strictly a business maxim, more a personal one: pay bills on time – never take on a casual debt.

One commercial lesson I recommend is how to handle joint ventures where each partner has a 50 per cent interest in such a venture. The principle is that, at any time, one of the partners is entitled to buy out the other partner's share by offering to buy that share at a price. The partner has two options; to accept or (if the price is deemed too low) to buy out the share of the offering partner at the price offered. It ensures that a fair price will be established. Just as when, according to Welsh custom, a child being offered half a piece of cake agrees: "You cut: I'll choose."

I often used pertinent quotations to keep everyone, including my peers, on their toes. In my last job, as Head of Corporate Communications, I was at pains always to ensure that keeping the company's reputation high was money well spent. Colleagues often feel that such activities are not cost effective, and sometimes suggest that they may be cut. I have quoted Menenius in which he justifies corporate overheads in the parable of the stomach:

There was a time when all the body's
      members
Rebelled against the belly, thus accused it:
That only like a gulf it did remain
I'the midst o' the body, idle and unactive,
Still cupboarding the viand, never bearing
Like labour with the rest...
... The belly answer'd –
'True is it, my incorporate friends,
That I receive the general food at first,
Which you do live upon;
... but, if you do remember,
I send it through the rivers of your blood,
... From me, receive that natural competency
Whereby they live..
... Though all at once cannot
See what I do deliver out to each,
Yet I can make my audit up, that all
From me do back receive the flour of all,
And leave me but the bran. [19]

Bran, it should be noted, is defined as the inedible part of grain, or, to use the OED definition: filth, excrement.

Most of my colleagues at BP, on retirement, became consultants either to BP, or to other companies in their own disciplines, including directorships. I was in the minority by not continuing in business after retirement and leaving my private finances to the Private Banking service of my bank. A quotation that fits this is of the about-to-be-cuckolded husband Pinchwife, in Wycherley's *The Country Wife*, to the supposed eunuch, Horner (which I played):

You go to your business, pleasure; while I go to my pleasure, business.

Well, the theatre is not all pleasure, but that's where I went.

Bottom

A Midsummer Night's Dream

"Take pains; be perfect; adieu"

THEATRE

The glamorisation of thought

In an interview Laurence Olivier, then director of the ten-year-old National Theatre, described the importance of theatre as the glamorisation of thought. It is a wonderful description. And the theatre has played an important part in my life. I believe that there is not a skill that cannot be used with advantage in the theatre. All participants have an equal responsibility to the success of the enterprise. Skills include design, lighting, stage management, sound, music, box office, front of house, computer skills, business management, costumes, make up, fight arranging, and many others to augment acting, dancing, singing and ensemble playing on stage. It is a truly democratic medium where the usual hierarchies of parent/child, boss/employee, rich/poor do not apply. And, in my case, the grandfather/grandchild relationship has also been equal and harmonious.

And it is my early experience in Shakespeare that provides most of the background to this personal testament of my theatre career.

It began with playing Lady Macbeth in a prep school production in a couple of scenes from *Macbeth*. At Bradfield I played Cassius in the open-air Greek theatre, which gave me my first real understanding of Shakespeare's genius and tempted me to think I was already a great actor. Arriving at Cambridge it soon became clear that, though able to hold my own in a Shakespeare play, I would be unlikely to be cast in major Shakespeare roles, so great was the talent and dedication of my contemporaries, even at that early stage of their careers.

In my final year the Marlowe Society production was *Alarums and Excursions*, a conflation of Parts 2 and 3 of *Henry VI*. Ian McKellen, now president of the Society, played the King and Michael Burrell, David Coombs and Anthony Arlidge were also in the cast, together with David Rowe-Beddoe, another distinguished actor who had also been busy in the theatre, though not so much involved with the Marlowe up to that point. David Rowe-Beddoe later became the driving force for building the Millennium Centre in Cardiff and was a cross-bench Peer in the House of Lords until his recent death.

My experiences of acting at Cambridge gave me far more than I might have expected. Cambridge at the time was the major classical theatre training of its day, at a time when the drama schools were getting more involved with the grittier contemporary fare of Osborne, Wesker and Whiting. The main vehicle for this was the Marlowe Society, which had been founded in 1908. One of its founders, Dadie Rylands, was still active while I was an undergraduate. The Marlowe Society was dedicated to the works of Shakespeare and his contemporaries, and mounted one or two productions each year at the Cambridge Arts Theatre. This had been founded by the economist John Maynard Keynes and was a professional venue, at which the Cambridge Footlights (led in my time by Peter Cook) also performed. I saw *Beyond The Fringe* at the Arts Theatre before it reached London, cementing Cook's fame with the others.

Dadie Rylands, a Don at King's College, had been a member of the Bloomsbury Set and promoted drama, particularly the Marlowe Society at Cambridge with Donald Beves. Rylands' greatest contribution to classical theatre was his emphasis on language. As a director, it is said, he sat with his eyes shut to concentrate on sound and meaning. And during the early 1960s he recorded the complete plays of Shakespeare for Argo, the record company who issued them for customers such as schools, universities and British Councils throughout the world. He used established actors, many of whom he had trained as undergraduates, giving the smaller parts to undergraduates of the day.

As a lecturer he performed great extracts of poetry – from *Paradise Lost* and *The Death of Doctor Swift* for example – performances of startling merit. As a reader in King's College Chapel he fed the words of the scriptures up the fluted columns of the chapel, where they lingered in a faint echo, achieved by a slower delivery that gave enough time for the sense to remain intact and to preserve their impressive sonority. In my second year he directed *Cymbeline* for the Marlowe Society. The cast was very strong; Margaret Drabble (the leading actress of her day) was Imogen, Derek Jacobi was Iachimo, Ian McKellen was Posthumous and Clive Swift was Cloten. I was approached before rehearsals began, not by Rylands himself, to take the small role of Jupiter which, even though his entry is on an eagle descending from the heavens, I turned down since Part I exams were nearing and my academic progress had not been helped by acting. As a result I could hardly complain that I was never asked to take part in the Argo recordings which is a slight regret, even today.

In my first year the Marlowe Society's main production was both parts of *Henry IV* directed by John Barton, a junior fellow who had taken over from Rylands and Beves as the main director of undergraduate theatre. He was a splendid actor and I well recall a production of Anouilh's *Antigone* in a College garden, in which he played Creon to Margaret Drabble's Antigone. When Peter Hall became director of the Royal Shakespeare Company, John Barton, a contemporary of Hall's at Cambridge, joined him at Stratford and later in London in a distinguished professional career. I particularly remember a wonderful production of *Peer Gynt* augmented by Norwegian folk songs. His main achievement at Stratford was in verse speaking, and examples of this were recorded for television and published as *Playing Shakespeare,* which remains crucial for any actor who wants to play Shakespearean roles properly.

In retrospect we were, I was, so lucky to have had him as our director and I learned more from him at that time than from any other individual. His production of these two plays is central to my theatrical experience.

It was all to a professional standard and we also had a taste of the professional theatre in such departments as design, costume and lighting, as well as acting in front of much larger audiences than previously. This professional training bore subsequent proof. The cast was full of talent: Falstaff was Clive Swift; Prince Hal was Derek Jacobi, a second-year undergraduate who had recently played Marlowe's Edward II at Edinburgh; Terrence Hardiman was Henry IV – all three went on to successful professional careers. Pistol was John Tydeman, who became head of BBC radio drama. In the newer intake were Simon Relph (Hotspur), a future head of BAFTA, John Wood (later Fortune) as Lord Chancellor, Corin Redgrave (Vernon), Anthony Arlidge (Worcester), Ian McKellen (Shallow) and Michael Burrell (Silence).

Michael Burrell's later career in the theatre was long and productive, without perhaps achieving household name status. When I retired, Michael was running a theatre company in Cambridgeshire and I got involved with him professionally for a few years there, playing King Duncan in *Macbeth*. My first professional performance was to a schools matinee audience. In the second half I came on as the Scottish doctor who watches Lady Macbeth in the sleepwalking scene, and subsequently reports back to Macbeth about her condition. As the lights went up I was in position looking upstage when a voice in the front row said, "I thought that bugger was dead." At least he had been paying attention to Act I.

Until his recent death, Michael Burrell and I cooperated on many theatrical projects including teaching at schools, filming Beckett, partaking in Christmas shows or celebrating the 700th anniversary of the granting of market status to Huntingdon. He was responsible for the King's Lynn Festival production, and in the Shallow and Silence scene he played Shallow and I played Silence. I also played Falstaff in a couple of extended excerpts.

Michael also directed me and Jules Melvin in the Doll Tearsheet scene, which we filmed in the George Inn in Southwark and is the closest I have come to achieving my ambition to play Falstaff. [QR1]

While Michael and Ian were constantly involved with plays at Cambridge, I was not as committed to the idea that my future profession might lie there. In my second year there was a production that was due to take its place in a student festival at Bristol, *The Revenger's Tragedy* by Cyril Tourneur. Richard Marquand, later a film director who died tragically young, took the lead: Vindice. David Coombs was Lussurioso and Derek Jacobi played Supervacuo, a part I was later to take.

I gained a real understanding of politics, too, from these plays. Much later in my business career I became responsible for Government Relations, among other duties, and I relied on a deep knowledge of the politics of these plays to guide me in that role. In my third year I played Humphrey, Duke of Gloucester, my most important role at Cambridge, whose advice to King Henry VI is pertinent:

> Ah, gracious lord these days are dangerous.
> Virtue is chok'd with foul ambition
> And charity chas'd hence by rancour's hand;

Foul subornation is predominant,
And equity exil'd your Highness' land. [20]

Prophetic words, unheeded in the play, and a significant political insight for modern times.

Humphrey, Duke of Gloucester
King Henry VI, Part II

After Cambridge in 1961, I joined BP at its international head-quarters in London. In 1962 I joined the Tower Theatre to continue my acting career. At that time the Tower had its own theatre in a magnificent Tudor building, Canonbury Tower. It produced about eighteen shows per year in the adjacent Edwardian Village Hall which, as a theatre, seated about 130. A typical production had an eight-week life – six weeks of rehearsal and eight performances over two weekends. Rehearsals took place in the wonderful Tudor rooms of the Tower from 7:30 each evening till 10 or 10:30, with Sundays from mid afternoon to early evening. As one show closed on a Saturday night the following show got in on the Sunday, when the set was built and lighting rigged. Monday was the technical rehearsal and two dress rehearsals followed before the opening on a Friday, followed by two performances on Saturday and one on Sunday. In the following week there were evening performances from Wednesday to Saturday.

This arrangement particularly suited me, living as I did in central London and with no business commitments after work or at the weekends. And since the Tower was only a few stops away from both the City and my home, it was possible to arrive on time and return home at a reasonable hour.

The advantage of this arrangement was that each show was together in one place at any one time, and the encounters in the buttery or in the bar of actors, directors, and the whole range of technical and design support fed off each others' experience and built relationships for future work together. And many went into the profession, making the quality of the company a further attraction. Another advantage of the Tower Theatre was that actors generally played within their natural age ranges.

My first audition at the Tower Theatre was for a part in *Arden of Faversham*. I had wanted to play Mosby, the lover of Mistress Arden, but was cast as Greene, one of the hapless would-be assassins. I nearly refused Greene, with the idea that I might look elsewhere with my talents. I'm very pleased I accepted, which began a long and happy relationship with the Tower.

Much later I realised that *Arden of Faversham* is an important play, which predates Shakespeare and prefigures three developments in theatre. These are:

a) Soliloquies
In what is an upper-middle-class domestic tragedy, there is no soliloquy for the eponymous hero, but no fewer than three given to Ralph, Arden's servant, who is talked into a plot to kill him, and debates the ethics of so doing.

b) Keystone cops
The various attempts to kill Arden arouse more humour than fear.

c) Whodunit?
The crime is discovered and the culprits punished owing to the evidence of the bloodstained footprints in the snow.

Shakebag, Greene and Black Will
Arden of Faversham

I did little acting at the Tower after Greene, turning my attention to directing. I must mention one role that I did get, the part of Shakespeare in Edward Bond's *Bingo*, a play I thought should have been called by its subtitle, "Scenes of Money and Death", on the last days of Shakespeare. This was a sombre piece, but I did discover that I could handle an important role (that Gielgud created) and do it justice. I can still see the pitcher as I drunkenly listened to Terry Marlowe as Ben Jonson, in the tavern scene – the motif on the pitcher *looking on me with lacklustre eye.* [21]

Shakespeare and Jonson, *Bingo*

Bingo came well after my first acting roles, since I began to direct plays soon after joining.

At Cambridge I had never been in the running to direct plays, though I did once consider asking Ian McKellen to play *Tamburlaine the Great* for me, but got no further than musing about it.

For the Tower's so-called Nursery productions I directed another double bill that was pretty eclectic, and was a success due in no small part to the willing participation of senior Tower actors, notably Bobbie Peacock, Edgar Davies and Fred Radley, who took leading roles in *The Second Shepherd's Play* by the Wakefield Master (which we played in the Old English Everyman edition version) and W. B. Yeats' *Calvary*. The Sheepstealer Mak became Judas, his wife became Mary and First Shepherd one of the chorus.

From that point on, for a few years, I became one of the busiest directors at the Tower:

- *Waiting for Godot* in 1963, a very early non-professional production with Fred Radley as a definitive Vladimir.

Vladimir and Estragon, *Waiting for Godot*

In 1964, in my late twenties, I was entrusted as a director to revive playing Shakespeare for Schools – this was a time when professional productions of Shakespeare were not as widespread as they are today. And I was greatly helped by some wonderful actors such as Walter Kennedy (who had been a member of Anew McMaster's Company in Belfast but was now, like me, engaged in business) and Margery Withers of the BBC (who later became a professional actress on the recommendation of Harold Pinter, who had seen her performance in the Tower's production of *The Birthday Party* and chose her for a television production of the same play). I directed, in fairly quick succession, productions of *Twelfth Night* (in which Walter Kennedy played Sir Toby and Gloria Dolskie, fresh from understudying Dorothy Tutin at Stratford, was Viola).

Sir Toby and Maria, *Twelfth Night*

1964 was Shakespeare's four hundredth anniversary, and also Christopher Marlowe's, his great contemporary.

I directed:

- *Tamburlaine the Great* – in 1964, perhaps only one of a few tributes to Marlowe's birthday, the two parts conflated to a three-hour-plus version with a cast of over thirty. David Rowe-Beddoe was magnificent in the title role, a production which features strongly in the chapter 'The Genius of Christopher Marlowe'.

Tamburlaine, Techelles and Zenocrate, *Tamburlaine the Great*

- *A Midsummer Night's Dream*

- *The Winter's Tale*

Clown, Mopsa, Autolycus and Dorcas, *The Winter's Tale*

In 1985 I directed *A Midsummer Night's Dream*, which we toured, with the same cast, with *The Winter's Tale*, to the antique Roman theatre in Arles en Provence in France. This was a major undertaking, more artistically rewarding than financially. The losses were heavy enough to cause our founder, Frank Smith, to make good, probably from his own pocket.

I directed two other Shakespeares in this period, *Macbeth* and *Romeo and Juliet*.

Juliet and Lady Capulet, *Romeo and Juliet*

- Ibsen's *Ghosts* – in which Bobbie Peacock played her final major role.

Mrs Alving and Pastor Manders, *Ghosts*

- *A Delicate Balance* by Edward Albee: Margery Withers, Valerie Testa, Walter Kennedy. Designed by David Taylor, his first show for the Tower.

Tobias and Agnes, *A Delicate Balance*

- *The Hot L Baltimore* – Lanford Wilson's lament for the great days of the railway and its hotels.

Jamie, April and Jackie, *The Hot L Baltimore*

I learned an important lesson as a director from Paul Rutledge, who was playing the night clerk: to take time rather than rushing into the action at the beginning of the play. I also needed a pizza box for a scene and got it in New York only after agreeing to pay for it with a pizza left uneaten. I also asked Lanford Wilson which song should be played at the end of the play: he recommended a Neil Sedaka number, "This will be our last dance together", which was indeed appropriate to the moment.

- *The King's Clown* by David Vando, a British premiere about the death of Molière with scenes from his plays.

In 1980 I received a call from Laurence Tuerk, who was my sound, lighting and filming colleague at the Tower, explaining that a director had dropped out of a production of Gorky's *Summerfolk* for the Cambridge University Players at the Minack Theatre and asked if I could take over. I suggested doing *The Comedy of Errors*, which is short, brilliant and far easier than *Summerfolk* to put on at short notice. It introduced me to Penny, his future wife who played Adriana, also of the BBC, who later became one of the dominant figures at the Tower, not only as actor, director, artistic director, but as Chairman and Chief Executive too. Penny and I co-directed a second production of *A Midsummer Night's Dream*, and I later played Prospero in her production of *The Tempest* amongst other ventures together. Both she and Laurence are outstanding examples of the contributions to theatre that such dedicated and talented non-professionals make.

Dromio of Syracuse, *The Comedy of Errors*

- I directed a Beckett triple bill of *Play*, *Come and Go* and *All That Fall* (in a radio version), which formed part of the conversation I had with Beckett in 1975, of which more later.

- *The Entertainer*, in which Terry Marlowe triumphed in the Olivier role of Archie Rice, notable among other things for the first nude lady on the Tower stage.

Bill Dudley, who later became a successful theatre designer, also did the set for a production of *Krapp's Last Tape* with Fred Radley, that started at London University. The original drawings by Bill of this were given to Beckett himself when I met him in Paris.

Being sent abroad on a posting interrupted work at the Tower. In New York, I did get involved with a similar semi-professional group called the CSC repertory company Off Off Broadway. My limited involvement consisted of:

- Assistant Director *Man and Superman*

- Assistant Director *Pericles*, where my main
  contribution was to suggest that Lysimachus
  should be played by the same actor as Pericles.

I was not available to act or direct at the Tower from 1980 to 1995, a period when I could not guarantee to be available for six–eight week periods due to my increasing seniority at BP. It was only a few years before I thought of retiring that I returned to play Blunt in Alan Bennett's *A Question of Attribution*, to see if I could still retain lines and perform to an adequate standard. Having satisfied myself that I could, I subsequently acted more meaty roles than hitherto and in plays that I considered to be important. These parts included:

Translations	Hugh the hedge-school teacher who speaks only Gaelic, Greek and Latin, a fabulous part in a great play, with this splendid ending: [P1]

Urbs antiqua fuit. There was an ancient city which 'tis said
Juno loved above all the lands. And it was the goddess's
    aim
and cherished hope that here should be the capital of all
nations – should the fates perchance allow that. [22] [QR2]

- *Action Against Sol Schulman*   A British premiere of which I was the eponymous hero, though having quite a small role.

- *Look Back in Anger*   Colonel Redfern, an ex-Imperial officer brimful of nostalgia for a long-lost life.

- *The Tempest*   Prospero in London and Paris, which Lily and Alana saw in both venues; my first major Shakespeare role since Cassius. (P5)

- *Uncle Vanya*   Serebryakov, accepted with a salute to Max Adrian. (P3)

- *Heartbreak House*   Shotover – a salute to Paul Scofield. (P2)

- *Waiting for Godot*   Pozzo, taking over from an actor who became indisposed at a late stage of rehearsal in my second production of the play. (P4)

- *Endgame*   Nagg encased in the dustbin, with Penny Tuerk as Nell. (QR3) (P8)

- *Marching Song*   Cadmus the pragmatic but morally questionable politician.

- *King Lear*   In London and Paris. (P6 & P7)

Lear
King Lear

The London run of *King Lear* was pretty successful in terms of performance and feedback. The shortened version works very well – 2½ hours including interval – and is not too demanding on either the cast or the audience, and the story drives along impressively, especially in such a small theatre as Theatro Technis. The audiences were healthy, given that Shakespeare at this level is not usually a crowd pleaser.

On a personal level I was pleased to have played the role, with some minor mistakes on occasion, and felt that all the preparation had been worthwhile and beneficial. I had more compliments than ever before for a combination of qualities – verse speaking, looks (four score and upward), variety, line retention and energy.

The wonderful writing is a huge help – blank verse and stunning language – and I felt that I gave everyone a fair account of the old man's decline.

Again on a personal note, I had organised a first night for friends of Michael Burrell, and had reserved seats "In memory of MB" to reflect our pact to have done *King Lear* together, with Michael playing the King and me Gloucester. Michael had been a junior member of the legendary Peter Brook Lear company and had learned much about this role from the great Paul Scofield.

Ian McKellen and David Rowe-Beddoe came, honouring his memory. Ian said to Sheila at the end, "Well, he need never act again," and he was most warm in his congratulations. "One note," he said. "In the storm scene you were being beaten by the elements; I think he was having fun at their expense and was actually enjoying the battering."

The family too were tremendous – Declan, Helena, Lily and Alana were full of praise. Owen flew in from Boston and came with two friends, recognising the personal importance of the play to me and applauding the age at which I managed to play it. My brother Philip and his family, Caroline, Michael and Toral, also came – Philip was about to play *Prince Lear*, a prequel, and said he now understood better what was in store for him.

More recently I have played

- *Dr Faustus* Old Man done in memory of Michael Burrell, whose last part this was.

And I appeared on my eightieth birthday, not for the Tower but for another London company, Sedos, in *You Can't Take it With You* – Grandpa.

My post-retirement parts are illustrations of the advantages of the non-professional – better parts than one could expect on the professional stage and no parts that one <u>has</u> to play even though one dislikes the role or the production. To have played Prospero and Lear in this time is supremely fulfilling for a Shakespearean like me.

After the same sixteen-year hiatus (1980–1995) while my jobs made me unavailable for any theatre activity, I directed a few more productions at the Tower, including:

- *A Midsummer Night's Dream* which I co-directed with Penny Tuerk and which went to Paris. Jill Batty was a splendid Titania/Hippolyta.

Oberon and Titania, *A Midsummer Night's Dream*

- *The Letters of Abélard and Héloïse*, at the request of Sara Randall, the Tower's long-serving Artistic Director, to re-establish the reputation of the author, Ronald Duncan, for his family. A fair shot at a neglected play. David Coombs played Abelard.

- *Waiting for Godot,* my second shot, to which Robert Gillespie and Ian McKellen came. I took over the part of Pozzo from Peter Novis.

My recent productions of Beckett's *Happy Days,* [P9] *Krapp's Last Tape, Play* and *All That Fall* have proved successful. *Happy Days* was memorable for the brilliance of Ruth Sullivan's performance, earning universally favourable reviews, including one from the Beckett Society. More of this in the Beckett chapter.

Today, the Tower Theatre, now located in its permanent home in Stoke Newington, continues to present a full programme of productions as it approaches its centenary year. Having been involved for over sixty years, I would like to record my thanks to all the artistic directors who have influenced me over the years: Clyde Jones, Ralph Shafran, Colin Ley, Penny Tuerk, Sara Randall, James Horne, Nigel Martin, Despina Sellar, Ella Slack, Colin Smith, Martin South, Martin Mulgrew and Ruth Sullivan. As well as Laurence Tuerk, Stephen Ley, John Dorsett, Tom Tillery, Jill Batty, John Morton and David Taylor. The legacy of the Tower's founders, Frank and Molly Smith, remains in robust health as the centenary approaches.

And my earlier point is valid here – one learns so much from colleagues in all the theatrical disciplines that enhances under-standing, appreciation and delight in the theatre. Seeing plays on a regular basis, and, in my case, writing a review of each perfor-mance, adds to this understanding.

I remain the longest serving Tower Director to this day.

≈

I have always considered myself to be a non-professional in the theatre; that is, I try to work to professional standards, and choose not to be paid for it. I should add, however, that on my retirement I applied for an Equity card to partake in professional productions. Michael Burrell helped me to obtain this for my work in *Macbeth* at the Angles Theatre in Wisbech, for which I received a fee. Thereafter I appeared in *Treasure Island* and *Hotel Bethlehem* for no fee. Later, my work with Robert Gillespie in *Oedipus Tyrannus* and its counterpoint, *Oedipus at the Crossroads*, and assisting with his production of *The Comedy of Errors* were also on a non-fee basis.

Fees I did earn came from playing Doctor Harold Shipman in a docudrama for Japanese television, and from a production I directed of *Butterflies Are Free*, which toured India to packed houses.

My most important directing (and co-producing) assignment was to adapt *Othello* in the Cyprus scenes for the Rosemary Branch Theatre under the title of *Black and White Sextet*.

The cast of six was equally split between black and white actors: Othello, Emilia and Rodrigo (a young Indian aristocrat with too much money) were black; Desdemona, Iago (with a black wife making his jealousy a degree worse) and Cassio were white. And 'Sextet' in the title hinted none too subtly at one of the dominant themes of the play.

To conclude this chapter. Professional theatre today is thriving in London, with major venues full of a wide variety of entertainments. Among these are musicals which generate great fortunes to all involved if successful. There are great modern companies providing a rich fare of classical and modern plays, the former keeping a strong theatrical tradition alive, the latter adding to that tradition for later times. There is a considerable range of local professional theatre for loyal audiences, whose best work is often promoted to major importance. And there is an even longer fringe, where new talent clamours for attention, promotion and sometimes, but rarely, achieves future fame and fortune.

The non-professional theatre provides an important role, particularly giving second productions of plays that are worth reviving, especially for younger audiences that may have missed the original productions.

All this theatrical richness demands much from those on both sides of the curtain. There may be periods of dullness, even boredom, but the highs of excitement and insight more than make up for the efforts involved. And Laurence Olivier's phrase with which I opened this chapter – the glamorisation of thought – captures this importance magnificently.

≈

The picture of Jack MacGowran (overleaf) is one of my most treasured possessions. It is a restored playbill from a New York production that I saw shortly before he died. He was one of Beckett's most trusted collaborators. This production, and Beckett's plays in general, also glamorised thought, however bleakly, though I detect humour and hope nonetheless. The green leaf of hope on the withered branch is a recurrent theme of these pages.

Onlooker beneath seven stars
The Poet and the Painter

THE SEVEN STARS PROJECTS

The reason why the seven stars are no more than seven is a pretty reason [23]

Since my retirement, now lasting thirty years, I have dedicated a separate bank account to my artistic projects, which I call my Seven Stars Projects Account. There has never been any expectation that these projects would make any serious money, quite the opposite: I expected to spend my discretionary cash on them. I even commissioned a seven-drawer bookcase for each of the projects at any one time. Several of these came to fruition over time and were written up accordingly. Others such as my acting and directing projects came and went as they were completed or abandoned. In rough order of starting, the following seven are perhaps the more satisfactory.

Three projects have achieved an extra life beyond these pages.

- Star I. *Meeting Samuel Beckett* is now in the Beckett archive of Reading University thanks to Professor James Knowlson, Beckett's biographer.

- Star II. *The Poet and the Painter* has been exhibited by the Royal Shakespeare Company and is currently on permanent loan to Shakespeare's Globe on Bankside.

- Star III. Publication of *First ACT Shakespeare*.

I hope that the original work of the other projects might too have an afterlife:

- Star IV. Further viewings of 'The Genius of Christopher Marlowe', with its distinguished cast, at the Rose Theatre, Bankside.

- Star V. The unmasking of the identity of 'A Gentleman of Cambridge', and particularly the quality of his prose.

- Star VI. A possible future production of *Pericles* involving ideas of casting, and the importance of the symbolism, in an adaptation called *Fathers and Daughters*.

- Star VII. A possible future professional performance of the four-voice version of *Four Quartets*.

Star I

Meeting Samuel Beckett

This account of my meeting Samuel Beckett dates from 1975, before my retirement. I include it as the first of my Seven Stars Projects. I wrote it immediately after our meeting and it remains important to me as one of my most successful achievements. This is what I wrote:

I suppose the main reason I wanted to meet Samuel Beckett was to flatter myself that I did shake hands with the writer who has written *the* play of the twentieth century. I believe I was seeking some kind of appreciation from him for what I have 'done' to his works, as if I deserved it or his works needed what I did.

I get the impression that the amount of attention he receives has rather amazed Beckett, not only because he had not perhaps expected to be famous in his lifetime but also because he had not expected to be used by remote acolytes imposing on his time. A generous man might not call it being used, and he is generous. A girl collecting for a children's charity sold him some unappealing postcards; I did not see anyone else buying.

From this innate generosity comes, no doubt, the conflicting statements of his agents, interpreters and others claiming his authority who variously report how Beckett wants his work performed. They may want to claim credit for being the true knowers of his real wishes, Beckett has no doubt been generous to them as well in the matter of his time, or they may be trying to provide a needed service in protecting him from people like me who keep asking.

I suspect Beckett needs such protection, though he seemed courteously at ease without it on this occasion. The matter is an enigma.

A second girl who I took to be his secretary arrived with a note for him, possibly a prearranged colour, to enable him to depart. He did not go.

How did this all arise in the first place? The photographs I sent him of my productions came close, I think, to what he had once imagined. He had always been friendly in his short acknowledgements, and when I asked to meet him he agreed. When I suggested a date when I would be in Paris he called me to confirm the appointment. The call was nearly lost in fact by my host denying to the calling Beckett the presence in his house of a Mr Jones.

The conversation when I finally reached the telephone was short, even abrupt. He named the Closerie des Lilas as if I should know it. It was, as I found out later, a famous meeting place of the artistic set in Paris in the twenties. He spelled it out letter by letter.

The unreality of the coming appointment weighed heavily. What right had I to his time; what common ground was there besides his published words; would he even come? I imagined the boy in Godot coming instead. I walked in an elegant formal garden for seven minutes to arrive precisely on time. But I was still too early. I sat on a bench for a minute and then saw him striding along precisely on the hour. I followed him in to the bar. We shook hands and he ordered Irish whiskey. I drank but did not taste beer.

My first glimpse of him at a distance had been of a tall

athletic figure walking with an easy paced stride (oh priceless gift of perfect timing), fit, lean and presumably tanned behind the dark glasses. Seated in the bar without the dark glasses he appeared older, but not seventy as he nearly is. He has close cropped grey hair, a scar from his glasses on his nose, clear but not hard blue eyes with a remote dreamy quality. His hands were those of an old man. He was dressed casually in a heavy white sweater and had taken off a light anorak. Why mention it, except that's what it was?

We, mainly I, talked of the plays, our only communication being the language of what he had written and the themes he had written about, all well documented theatrical details which add nothing to knowledge. The framework was of a factual and theatrical nature. Did you see? ... Yes I did ... What about? ... No I was out of town, sort of thing.

He has been directing a good deal lately, in Berlin, in London (*Happy Days* with Peter Hall) and now in France (*Not I* and *Krapp's Last Tape*). I said that the ending of *Happy Days* in London – Willie's outstretched hand, small gap, revolver pointing at Winnie, small gap, Winnie's imprisoned head – had been a good deal clearer than it was in the Madeleine Renaud production. He seemed pleased; perhaps he had suggested the clarification himself.

I asked if he enjoyed directing and he said that his greatest preoccupation was with movement and the stage mechanics rather than the words. He thought he knew what the words all meant. But no he didn't particularly enjoy directing. I suspect it cuts into his other time.

Thinking of *Waiting for Godot*, the play that gives the director most discretion in regard to movement, I recalled one moment where a stage direction seemed wrong (the incident involves Pozzo). He could not agree though he mentioned some imprecision with regard to Lucky's rope at one of the exits. The stage directions of *Krapp's Last Tape* have some small imprecisions and Beckett is reissuing a text with appropriate revisions. I could not remember any such problem with this play but I remembered the awkwardness of lifting off both reels of tape (to avoid a long rewind and wind-on). In both instances our experiences of directing the play seem different.

Of his current project, directing, or helping to direct, Madeleine Renaud in *Not I*, he mentioned having had difficulty in translating the English into French. He also told of the device whereby Billie Whitelaw had maintained contact with the stage manager in the London production, to overcome the totality of isolation that would otherwise have existed. Apparently she had an earphone connection with the stage manager. If she needed a prompt she had pre-arranged a special word sequence that would serve to alert the stage manager that she had lost her way. I made a banal remark that there was additional support afforded her by the Auditor. The actress can of course see nothing, and the impact of the Auditor's support or lack of it is entirely for the audience.

Billie Whitelaw had been perfect for the role and Beckett, who remembered her in *Play*, had asked the director specifically for her, she not being the director's first choice. He also recommended that Jack Emory (who by this time had joined us, of whom more later) use Billie Whitelaw in the project that he was outlining. He mentioned how happy he was that her child had recovered from an illness, another sympathetic instance.

Of interest too in his current project was the fact that a young actor was playing Krapp in the double bill with *Not I*. Beckett thought that the actor's age was not important, believing the skill of the actor concerned was enough. I said I thought an older actor was altogether preferable but forgot Krapp's exact age which is, as Beckett quickly noted, sixty-nine. He had not been impressed by Albert Finney in the part, thinking he had not committed himself to the full. I also got the impression that despite the present plan he felt *Krapp's Last Tape* to be an unsuitable partner for *Not I* in a double bill. *Play* was mentioned as being more suitable.

He has practically completed a new play in the same series as *Play* and *Not I*. It will be performed at the Royal Court next year when a retrospective of Beckett's work is to be given. Beckett has a loyalty to the Royal Court dating from George Devine's days. The new play – to be called, I think, *That Time* (I contracted the title in my mind to *Then*, muttered it and got an odd look) – is to be about twenty minutes in length. It would I suppose be another of Beckett's experiments of stripping away an accepted theatrical dimension. I gathered that the audience will see an old man's head suspended in space, he not speaking.

I pointed out the obvious similarity to *Eh Joe*, which Beckett acknowledged with more than a hint of resignedness that all his pieces tend to an eventual similarity. Several times my eagerness in noting similarities seemed, if not to hit a raw nerve, at least to sadden him somewhat. The writing of *That Time* (in English) is finished, the attendant stage mechanics (movement?) not settled.

Of my own projects of the moment that of *Lessness* occupied most of the time. I asked him whether six voices or one should be used. The Beckett exhibition handbook quotes the six-voice arrangement as having been communicated by the author to John Calder. However, Martin Esslin said that Beckett had changed his mind since Esslin had used the six-voice arrangement in the radio production. Beckett recalled that the piece was indeed written for six voices or rather that it had six themes of twelve sentences each and that once each had been stated, each theme was repeated in a different order. My own research had isolated six themes though not quite the right ones. What I had not established was (a) the exactness of the repeat – I had made two charts which looked practically identical but which I had not by then finally proved to be exact duplicates and (b) which the precise groups were, owing to the merging of the key descriptive ideas; for example, greyness is not confined to the wilderness theme. Two minutes of conversation clarified these points entirely and I wondered where the difficulty had been. It was interesting to note that Beckett's memory was slightly defective in that there are only ten statements, not twelve, about each of the six themes, as if that mattered. The important point was that the six-voice treatment was endorsed.

I explained, badly I expect, my idea of underlining the internal colouring of the six groups, i.e. allowing the dominant image of each theme to overlap into other themes, giving each sentence to the theme voice and adding one or more 'colouring' voices, which would repeat echoes of their themes whenever these echoes appeared in other theme statements. Beckett looked doubtful and I did not pursue. I knew, however, that I could now easily pick out the themes, and I resolved to try my idea of the multi-voiced approach in the repeat half at least.

As to what I had done in the past, I told him of *All That Fall* as a 'radio' experience in a theatre. He was most interested about the mechanics of this, but asked if the actors were visible and seemed surprised when I told him they were not. Remember I had received particular instructions from the agents quoting Beckett's authority that actors were *not* to be visible. So his surprise this day was a surprise to me as well.

I told him of the recreation on film of the convention of the sustained scrutiny of Joe, in *Eh Joe*, and confessed the one break I had to make. Again he expressed real interest and, probably more out of politeness than anything else, said he would like to see it some time, though not in Paris this time.

I talked of *Come and Go* and Martyn Corbett spending half his review of a three-play bill on the tiny piece, and how Mimi Woodford in a part of a dozen lines only had nevertheless the habit of calling the others by her own or the third character's name.

I talked of the problem of ensuring that the light exactly hit the middle urn in *Play*. Beckett did not instantly see that it would be impossible to stop the lantern centrally with a device like a bar (as was used for the outside urns). Such a bar would prevent the lantern from continuing its progress to the outside urns to the left or right.

With regard to *Krapp's Last Tape* I told him how I demanded that Fred Radley, the actor, find the exact place on the tape for the run ons and run backs though, as I since learned, the trick is to wire the tape deck in the sound box to the tape recorder's own speaker, obviating the need for any exact rewinding by the actor.

All in all he expressed surprise at how much I had done. I believe I mentioned *Tamburlaine* and *A Delicate Balance* too.

As a slight effort to contribute a creative idea I mentioned that I thought him to be a numbers man, that he understands their subtle interactions and uses them with a greater effect than most. I think of the stones, the steps in *All That Fall:*

"Not count! One of the few satisfactions in life." [24]

the angles in *Film* and so on. I mentioned the first time I noticed it, the afterthought in Krapp's:

"One pound six and something, eight I have little doubt." [25]

"Oh the old solicitor's fee" was his comment. However, apart from admitting a rudimentary knowledge of arithmetic and agreeing, smiling, that he once played cricket, the game with the life rhythm but dominated with numbers, he did not seem to agree with the theory to any extent. I persevered by wondering if a play could be written not in words but in numbers only, but the idea appeared not to catch fire.

He made an interesting comment about *Film*, that the concept was a mixture of two perspectives of the same incident, that of the fugitive and of the pursuer. The two perspectives were supposed to have been differentiated by a change in the intensity of the focus which was to have been achieved by the use of gauze over the camera's lens. The difference between the two intensities had not been achieved clearly enough in the event.

I had suggested that *Mercier and Camier* was suitable for a film treatment, I thought of the scenario like chapter summaries. The locations are specific and the incidental nature of the piece seemed suitable for such treatment. Beckett merely added that much of the material in the novel had been used in *Waiting for Godot*.

He seems to distrust film, or is it film makers? He cited a film version of *Waiting for Godot* and complained that studios tend to indulge in excessive use of close-ups and other distorting technical tricks. The only acceptable treatment of

Waiting for Godot for example would be a recording of a stage production from a single fixed viewpoint. I believe his recent West Berlin production was being so recorded.

Perhaps he would never see the film since he never goes to his own shows ('I am too nervous'). Indeed he hardly ever goes to the theatre at all, though he did admit to having been impressed (partly) with the Peter Brook *Lear*.

Fast running out of the obvious conversational points, I moved on to what I might do one day. I wondered if the music for *Words and Music* by John Beckett was an integral part of that text. The music has remained unpublished. Beckett said that his cousin considers it unsuccessful and thus will not publish. Any new production is therefore to be given a new musical treatment.

At this point I mention Mr Emory again. He was my idea of what I suppose is worst in all of us hangers on, and he looked like it too, a bardic looking young Krapp with the outward trappings of Lucky. And yet having done a one-man Beckett show in places like Adelaide and Edinburgh, he probably had more right than I to be there. But had he? His credentials were obscure. He had done Eng. Lit. and for his PhD had studied Beckett to find a link between the novels and the plays. Finding none, had been persuaded to put the research to use in the form of a one-man show.

On this occasion he was looking for unpublished material which he could use exclusively (of course!) in a planned tour of Beckett plays to be performed in repertory. He named names like Scofield, Max Wall (of whom Beckett had not heard) and Harold Pinter (to direct). Beckett was most courteous to him as well and mentioned the Royal Court retrospective next year at which all the plays and the new one are to be mounted (Emory had not heard of this). Beckett recommended Patrick Magee and Billie Whitelaw as artists. A possible work for first time theatrical exploitation was *Texts for Nothing*, he said.

I mentioned earlier his attachment to the Royal Court. He clearly has lasting loyalties. Two other incidents impressed this on me. First in his preference for using actors he likes and understands such as Billie Whitelaw and Patrick Magee (for whom he wrote *Krapp's Last Tape* having at that time heard his voice only on the radio, not having met him). Preeminent among those trusted interpreters was Jack MacGowran, whose sudden death had obviously hit him hard. He recounted the details of that last season in New York. MacGowran had been giving the one-man Beckett show *Beginning to End* (which thank goodness I had taken the opportunity to see at that time). He followed this by rehearsing for a production of *Juno and the Paycock* when he collapsed and died. A couple of times I noticed a real sadness when Beckett talked of him. Finally, he had obviously been pleased at the success of Joyce's *Exiles* at the RSC, noting that it must have been the first proper production of the piece since Joyce wrote it.

His attitude to what is not so close to him was to be helpful in a general way, which brings me to wonder whether I am right in thinking he needs protection from enthusiasts and exploiters of his work. At one moment he was mentioning who exactly was to be consulted on business matters, yet in the next breath he was asking us if there was anything he could do for us. Despite his and others' best endeavours he seems to leave himself just that much more available than his precautions would seem to seek to prevent.

I recall his pleasure at aptness. Indeed a smile of approbation, a sudden brightening of his intense blue eyes, was really *the* moment for me. Emory had been recounting how on arriving in Australia after a day-long flight, he had taken a bath and the depressurisation effect, or whatever, had caused his feet to swell so much that he could not put on his shoes. I noted "There's mankind for you, blaming on his boots the faults of his feet" [26] – a reaction of pure joy from Beckett.

The exit was pure Beckett too. At the next table had just sat down with difficulty an old man with a stiff leg – shades of Molloy – and his stiff leg was resting alongside a chair. He was being hand fed by a female companion, and he had dribbled some of the food on his chin. The situation was really very apt. I had given Beckett a picture of Fred as Krapp that Bill Dudley had done for me.

He gathered this up, still wrapped in brown paper, together with his anorak and his briefcase. Beckett, now loaded like Lucky, said goodbye and in extricating himself from behind our table succeeded in knocking over the chair against which the old man's injured leg was resting.

If the impression of the above is of an action-packed encounter, it is a false impression. Beckett spoke softly, with a pleasant Irish brogue. I was deferential. One or two silences descended as the basic unreality of the meeting made itself felt. Having now met him, I would love to know him better, but this is impossible from all points of view. To have met him once will have to be and is enough.

My subsequent Beckett career includes:

- *Stones* – This passage from *Molloy* has obsessed me ever since I saw Jack MacGowran perform it in New York. As well as filming Michael Burrell on Worthing beach, I have also recorded it on film, which can be accessed via YouTube. [QR4]

- *Eh Joe* – The re-dubbing by Penny Tuerk of the film Laurence Tuerk and I made with Fred Radley and Margery Withers.

- *Krapp's Last Tape* – My own performance on film directed by Penny Tuerk and shot by Stephen Ley has much to commend it and it is something that I hope will be valid in years to come for small audiences. I love this from the play:

Seventeen copies sold, of which eleven at trade price to free circulating libraries across the seas.
Getting known. One pound six and something, eight I have little doubt. [27]

- *Waiting for Godot* – my second production re-emphasised my interpretation (and that of others) that Vladimir and Estragon represent the Mind and the Body, joined together but in an uneasy relationship. This duality of opposites is echoed in most of the other manifestations: master/slave; sheep/goats; you/your brother; fair .. or black?; one of the thieves was saved; leaves/barren branches; sighted/blind; garrulousness/dumbness and so on. But I did finally work out that Act II has something of a detective story in it, in that Vladimir has five attempts at proving to Estragon that they had come back to the same place as they had been the previous day. The five bits of evidence are:

  > The tree (though now covered in leaves)
  > The festering wound from Lucky's kick
  > The boots
  > The mound where Estragon slept
  > Lucky's hat

One of the greatest challenges for an actor is Lucky's speech. I have not been able to help the actor very much with how he should play it and it is now, after two efforts, that I tentatively offer the idea that the six main strands of the speech are:

Personal God

Given the existence of   Who loves us dearly   For reasons unknown

The world's distractions

Feckham, Peckham   In spite of the tennis   The stones

Fates of mankind

The skull   Wastes and pines   Great cold

Authority of others

Puncher and Wattman   Cunard   Bishop Berkeley

Lucky's comments

But time will tell   And who can doubt it

Lucky's speech structure

That is to say   But not so fast   What is more

It may help if the various strands of his thoughts are identified by (say) a slightly different intonation. It is marvellous theatre, however it is played.

- *Endgame* – The experience of playing Nagg but also my insistence that Clov's line at the end of the prayer sequence when Hamm ejaculates
  The bastard! He doesn't exist. [28]

is to add the cautionary

Not yet. [29]

In one of the editions these two words are omitted.

And finally to highlight the masterful conclusion
to Winnie's Day.

… This will have been another happy day!

After all.

So far. [30]

One of the keys to Winnie's performance, which Ruth Sullivan
played so brilliantly, is to agree the different intonations of her
voice which include:

Diminishing optimism
Making sense of her predicament
Daily routine and the toothbrush
Mobility
Suburban values
State of marriage
Concern for Willie
Scorn of Willie (including his voice parody)
Charlie Hunter and the first kiss
Reminiscence (tool shed)
Story of Millie
Mr Shower (Ruth's brilliant suggestion of
Birmingham accent)
Mrs Shower
Her quotations from literature

There is also the equivocation of the final moments as the revolver comes into play.

Equivocation of the revolver – to use it or not, by whom on whom?

More recently I directed my second production of *Krapp's Last Tape* with John Chapman at the Tower Theatre. And in 2023 I directed my second *Play* and *All That Fall*, the radio play, performed live as I had done before, with the late Linda Shannon playing Maddy, shortly before her untimely death. John Chapman played Dan, her husband, who, in the play, considers the following sermon:

How to be Happy Though Married [31]

Unhappily, in 2024 John Chapman died; another tragic loss.

With my granddaughter Alana we completed performances for YouTube of the Stones sequence from Beckett's novel *Molloy*; and his short play *That Time*, for which I had impertinently offered Beckett an alternative title – *Then* – all those years before.

I opened my account of meeting with Beckett with the remark that I wanted my grandchildren to know that I had met the greatest playwright of the twentieth century. I had no grandchildren at that time, but Alana, now recently graduated, played a vital role in *Happy Days*, operating Stephen Ley's superb lighting and sound creation, so there is a hope that Alana's grandchildren may in time stretch out the connection to a significant extent.

I must record my recent involvement with the Samuel Beckett archive at Reading University. Professor Emeritus James Knowlson, Beckett's biographer with the wonderful *Damned to Fame*, has been most supportive in placing some of my Beckett records in the archive.

To conclude I repeat others' examples of his wit which deserve a second outing:

> Young girl (racing after Beckett): Mr. Beckett, Mr. Beckett, I have read all your works.
> Samuel Beckett: You must be very tired.

Matthew Warchus, in a programme note, writes:

> When Beckett was working on a play at the Royal Court ... he arrived at the rehearsal room one sunny, blue-skied morning and declared: "Ah, it's a beautiful day today". "Yes", one of the cast replied "It makes you glad to be alive". "Well, I wouldn't go that far" said Beckett.

And this, from *How It Is*:

> Nothing like breathing your last to put new life in you. [32]

As one who suffers what the late Dame Thora Hird described as "the aches and pains we all get from time to time," I am suitably heartened by this quotation. Wham. Bam. Thank you, Sam.

The Poet and the Painter
Timon of Athens

Star II

The Poet and the Painter

Perhaps my most lasting and important contribution was to commission Ronnie Copas, an artist and friend, to paint my retirement present to myself. This was to be a picture of a defining moment from each of Shakespeare's plays, chosen by me. Ronnie would be free to interpret the task, painting one picture of thirty-seven moments or thirty-seven of one, or any other combination in between. In the event he opted for the former, rebuilding his studio to accommodate the 6 ft x 9 ft masterpiece called *The Poet and the Painter*.

This picture was originally exhibited by the Royal Shakespeare Company at Stratford, and it subsequently toured to Newcastle, Plymouth and King's Lynn. It hung in my home until, in 2016, I presented it to Shakespeare's Globe Theatre in London where it now hangs. A wonderful photographic reproduction now hangs on my walls with no loss of quality. I produced a catalogue for those exhibitions with this introduction:

I visited Belgium a few years ago with my wife, Sheila. We went to Ghent to see *The Adoration of the Lamb*, the Van Eyck brothers' masterpiece dating from 1432.

We happened to choose a Saturday in November. The morning was dismal: cold, dark, rainy, raw. Little wonder the streets around the cathedral, where the painting is housed, were deserted. We arrived early – the cathedral was not due to open until 10 o'clock – so we found the only cafe open and had a coffee. Five minutes before the hour we left the cafe. As we walked the few yards to the great West Door, we saw, emerging from every street and alleyway that ran into the square, couples and single figures, people on the same mission as us, strolling towards the cathedral. There must have been a small crowd of thirty or forty when 10 o'clock struck and the doors opened.

What pulling power! Here was a picture, painted 550 years ago, attracting an audience from all over the world to a quiet town in Belgium, even on such an unpropitious day. But when we saw the picture we could understand why. This is not the place to discuss Van Eyck except to say that whenever I have been within 100 miles of the painting I make a detour to see it; it was, in part, the inspiration for this project.

The Poet

Shakespeare exerts a tremendous power too. Just one small personal example. In 1986, I was flying on business to Malaysia and had a copy of *King Lear* with me. There, at a height of 30,000 feet, over the Maldive Islands, some 7,000 miles from London, and 380 years after it was written, I came across this:

> Lear: How old art thou?
> Kent: Not so young, sir, to love a woman for singing, nor so old to dote on her for anything. I have years on my back forty-eight. [33]

That hit home, even at such a distance of space and time from when it was first written. I was forty-eight and I completely recognised Kent's sentiments as my own.

Shakespeare does that. Even when you are listening to or reading the most familiar passage of a play, he has the capacity to surprise with new insight or nuance.

As noted, I have been lucky enough to direct Shakespeare in the theatre, to act him and to have seen hundreds of productions, completing the canon with *Timon of Athens* in 1991. I read him too, especially on long journeys. Recently I did a series of broadcasts for the BBC World Service on defining moments in Shakespeare. I have even taught him in school. In short, I am a Shakespeare enthusiast, some might even say fanatic!

Upon taking early retirement from the international oil industry in 1994, I determined to continue and intensify my involvement with the theatre and with Shakespeare. I also had the once-in-a-lifetime opportunity to commission a major work of art, thanks to BP's generous retirement terms. By major, I mean something that would endure long after my lifetime. Perhaps I could never expect it to have the 'pulling' power of an *Adoration of the Lamb* or a *King Lear* but I wanted it to be something which future generations could look at and enjoy. There was no doubt in my mind that Shakespeare would be the subject.

So, I had my poet and I knew that my commission would be a painting, for I had the painter too. The title, *The Poet and the Painter*, was to come later.

The Painter

Sheila and I had known Ronnie Copas and his wife, Liz, for more than fifteen years and I had been buying his paintings for somewhat longer. He is not only a great artist but also a great friend. He was the obvious choice to paint this picture.

The Project

In June 1994, I invited Ronnie to our little house overlooking most of Greenwich reach, to sound him out about helping me celebrate my passion for Shakespeare. I wrote in my diary of our meeting:

"My own idea is for a major painting, maybe a triptych, celebrating Shakespeare's genius in which a scene from each of his plays would be depicted. My input would be to select the crucial scenes from the plays – the 'defining moments' as I call them – moments such as 'Exit pursued by a bear'. I would also direct the overall 'staging' of each dramatic situation and theme. Ronnie would be responsible for how it looked on the canvas technically, and for the decisions on, for example, costume and characters.

"I felt he was not certain of the technical solution and unmoved by the vision. He made some prosaic counterproposals, which may be no less achievable. In 'thinking about it' I fear he may be thinking how to break his lack of enthusiasm for it."

One thing we did agree was that we would leave the rest of the year so that both of us could reflect further on the project. It would have been disastrous to have rushed into it without careful thought about both the potential and the problems.

Ronnie took a couple of months to overcome his initial reserve and to decide that we might be able to pull it off after all. I wrote to him, saying that because his response had not been a "Eureka!" but was instead considered and constructive, it was all the more valuable for that. "The idea is worth the investment in our abilities, time and cash that we are contemplating. I would love to have a go," I told him.

The Project's Progress

In the late summer of 1994, I began the task of choosing the incidents from the thirty-seven plays. I sent these to Ronnie, with a scribbled sketch as to how I saw each incident, in terms of staging it. Sheila coped patiently with the long process of drafting the notes I made to accompany every selection.

At this point, Ronnie's health was becoming a problem. It had been caused by a wretched piece of luck over a prescription for steroids that were supposedly to heal one complaint but in fact served only to harm him permanently. It was a very worrying time for him, his family and his friends. Despite this setback, Ronnie stoically began in January 1995 what became a year's work – supplying the individual drawings.

An open question at this time was whether there would ultimately be one canvas of thirty-seven incidents, or thirty-seven separate canvases each depicting a single incident, or some intermediate solution.

The installation of fax machines at our two houses helped to speed up the process. It was also, for me, a wonderful medium for the 'birth' of each of Ronnie's ideas. As I waited, like a nervous father, the fax machine would issue the drawing, as if a child from the womb. I would scan the newly born baby with a quick anticipation, eager to see the new miracle.

By October, the underpainting completed, Ronnie had begun his work on painting each scene in its final form. It was at this time that I hit on the title. I was having a second look at the dialogue between the Poet and the Painter in *Timon of Athens*, having more or less decided it was that incident in that play which would provide a suitable title page for this book. It was these lines which convinced me:

Poet: Let's see your piece.
Painter: 'Tis a good piece.
Poet: So 'tis; this comes off well and excellent.
Painter: Indifferent.
Poet: Admirable… I will say of it,
It tutors Nature; artificial strife
Lives in these touches, livelier than Life. [34]

In those last lines, Shakespeare defines Ronnie's actual style of painting. Yet another example of his stupendous reach! So *The Poet and the Painter* it was. I was already The Patron, and the project was The Project.

The painting was finished on Friday, March 21, 1997, one thousand and three days since I had first mentioned the idea.

The final contribution was the specially designed frame by Derek Beard, master cabinet-maker from Burnham-on-Sea.

In my business career, I always found it satisfying to devise a project and then to see it through to a successful conclusion. To be able to do the same with a major work of art is a very special privilege. Ronnie Copas, Liz, Sheila and I have drawn great enjoyment from the whole process, from conception to birth. Our hope is that all who see it, both now and in years to come, will feel that our labours were worth the looking on.

The illustration of *The Poet and Painter* on p.95 includes reference numbers for each play's defining moment. The particular scenes of each play are given here in the order of these numbers, together with a short red-letter quotation. The illustrated detail with full quotation and note can be accessed here:

1 MACBETH
Act 2, Scene 1, Line 1
How Goes the Night, boy? (QR5)

2 KING JOHN
Act 4, Scene 1, Line 28
Are you sick, Hubert? you look pale today: (QR6)

3 HAMLET
Act 3, Scene 2, Line 23
..., to hold, as 'twere, the mirror up to nature; (QR7)

4 KING HENRY V
Act 1, Scene 2, Line 35
There is no bar
To make against your highness' claim to France (QR8)

5 KING HENRY VI, PART I
Act 2, Scene 5, Line 73
I was the next by birth and parentage; (QR9)

6 ROMEO AND JULIET
Prologue, Line 5
A pair of star-cross'd lovers (QR10)

7 THE COMEDY OF ERRORS
Act 5, Scene 1, Line 250
... Till, gnawing with my teeth my bonds in sunder, (QR11)

8 KING HENRY VI, PART II
Act 4, Scene 6, Line 1

I charge and command that, of the city's cost, the pissing-conduit run nothing but claret wine this first year of our reign. (QR12)

9 THE TWO GENTLEMEN OF VERONA
Act 2, Scene 3, Line 34

Now the dog all this while sheds not a tear nor speaks a word… (QR13)

10 THE MERRY WIVES OF WINDSOR
Act 2, Scene 1, Line 55

I shall think the worse of fat men (QR14)

11 CORIOLANUS
Act 1, Scene 1, Line 153

What do you think
You, the great toe of this assembly? (QR15)

12 ALL'S WELL THAT ENDS WELL
Act 1, Scene 1, Line 74

Love all, trust a few,
Do wrong to none: (QR16)

13 ANTONY AND CLEOPATRA
Act 5, Scene 2, Line 305

With thy sharp teeth this knot intrinsicate
Of life at once untie: (QR17)

14 KING HENRY IV, PART I
Act 2, Scene 4, Line 528
… banish plump Jack, and banish all the world.
Prince: I do, I will. (QR18)

15 KING HENRY VIII
Act 3, Scene 2, Line 352
The third day comes a frost, a killing frost... (QR19)

16 KING RICHARD III
Act 3, Scene 4, Line 31
I saw good strawberries in your garden…
I do beseech you send for some of them. (QR20)

17 THE TAMING OF THE SHREW
Act 2, Scene 1, Line 247
Why does the world report that Kate doth limp? (QR21)

18 PERICLES
Act 5, Scene 1, Line 85
She speaks
My lord, that, may be, hath endured a grief
Might equal yours, (QR22)

19 THE TEMPEST
Act 5, Scene 1, Line 50
And deeper than did ever plummet sound,
I'll drown my book. (QR23)

20 THE WINTER'S TALE
Act 3, Scene 3, Line 58

[Exit pursued by a bear] (QR24)

21 CYMBELINE
Act 4, Scene 2, Line 258

Fear no more the heat o' th' sun, (QR25)

22 KING LEAR
Act 1, Scene 5, Line 38

The reason why the seven stars are no more than seven is a pretty reason. (QR26)

23 TROILUS AND CRESSIDA
Act 3, Scene 3, Line 169

O let not virtue seek
Remuneration for the thing it was; (QR27)

24 JULIUS CAESAR
Act 4, Scene 3, Line 63

Do not presume too much upon my love;
I may do that I shall be sorry for. (QR28)

25 KING HENRY VI, PART III
Act 2, Scene 5, Line 42

Gives not the hawthorn bush a sweeter shade
…
To kings that fear their subjects' treachery? (QR29)

26 AS YOU LIKE IT
Act 3, Scene 2, Line 83

If thou be'st not damned for this, the devil himself will have no shepherds: (QR30)

27 LOVE'S LABOUR'S LOST
Act 5, Scene 2, Line 938

The words of Mercury are harsh after the songs of Apollo. You, that way: We, this way. (QR31)

28 KING HENRY IV, PART II
Act 3, Scene 2, Line 36

Shallow: Death is certain. Is old Double of your town living yet?

Silence: Dead, sir.

Shallow: Jesu! Jesu! Dead! (QR32)

29 MUCH ADO ABOUT NOTHING
(i) Act 2, Scene 3, Line 108 (ii) Act 3, Scene 1, Line 107

Is't possible? Sits the wind in that corner?

What fire is in mine ears? Can this be true? (QR33)

30 KING RICHARD II
Act 3, Scene 4, Line 104

Here did she fall a tear; here in this place,
I'll set a bank of rue…
In the remembrance of a weeping queen. (QR34)

31 TITUS ANDRONICUS
Act 4, Scene 2, Line 98
Coal black is better than another hue, (QR35)

32 A MIDSUMMER NIGHT'S DREAM
Act 1, Scene 2, Line 100
Take pains; be perfect; adieu. (QR36)

33 THE MERCHANT OF VENICE
Act 1, Scene 3, Line 20
… there be land-rats, and water-rats, land-thieves, and water-thieves, (I mean pirates)… (QR37)

34 MEASURE FOR MEASURE
Act 3, Scene 2, Line 187
… this ungenitured agent will unpeople the province with continency. (QR38)

35 TWELFTH NIGHT
Act 4, Scene 2, Line 134
Pare thy nails, dad,
Adieu, goodman devil! (QR39)

36 OTHELLO
Act 2, Scene 3, Line 29
Well happiness to their sheets! Come, lieutenant, I have a stoup of wine… (QR40)

37 TIMON OF ATHENS
Act 1, Scene 1, Line 36
It tutors Nature; artificial strife
Lives in these touches, livelier than Life. (QR41)

1. *Macbeth*
2. *King John*
3. *Hamlet, Prince of Denmark*
4. *The Life of King Henry V*
5. *The First Part of King Henry VI*
6. *Romeo and Juliet*
7. *The Comedy of Errors*
8. *The Second Part of King Henry VI*
9. *The Two Gentlemen of Verona*
10. *The Merry Wives of Windsor*
11. *Coriolanus*
12. *All's Well That Ends Well*
13. *Antony and Cleopatra*
14. *The First Part of King Henry IV*
15. *The Famous History of the Life of King Henry VIII*
16. *The Tragedy of King Richard III*
17. *The Taming of the Shrew*
18. *Pericles, Prince of Tyre*
19. *The Tempest*
20. *The Winter's Tale*
21. *Cymbeline*
22. *King Lear*
23. *Troilus and Cressida*
24. *Julius Caesar*
25. *The Third Part of King Henry VI*
26. *As You Like It*
27. *Love's Labour's Lost*
28. *The Second Part of King Henry IV*
29. *Much Ado About Nothing*
30. *The Tragedy of King Richard II*
31. *Titus Andronicus*
32. *A Midsummer Night's Dream*
33. *The Merchant of Venice*
34. *Measure for Measure*
35. *Twelfth Night, or, What You Will*
36. *Othello, The Moor of Venice*
37. *Timon of Athens*

First ACT
Shakespeare

Illustrated by

Clive
Francis

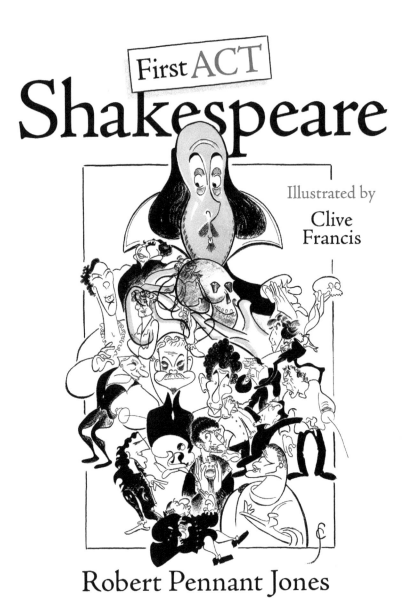

Robert Pennant Jones

Star III

First ACT Shakespeare

In the late nineties I did some research into the relative popularity of Shakespeare's plays under the title of 'The Seven Stars'. The research led to my writing a book I called *The Shakespeare Pack*, which was not published, though much of the material was included in *First ACT Shakespeare*, published in 2021. Brief accounts of these follow.

THE SHAKESPEARE PACK

Robert Pennant Jones

Illustrated by Clive Francis

The Seven Stars

The Seven Stars was an attempt to measure the popularity of Shakespeare's plays (from 1964 to 1995).

The Shakespeare Pack used the rankings of the Seven Stars in a draft of an ambitious effort with text, illustrations, recordings and cruxes to produce a significant handbook for 16- to 25-year-olds embarking on a Shakespeare career. It was unpublished, but revised as *First ACT Shakespeare*.

Ultimately, of course, ranking works of art is a sterile exercise. We should simply be glad we have the thirty-seven plays, in this case, and not agonise too much about selecting our favourite seven. Yet the very act of choosing one play rather than another forces us to consider its particular merits in context. So even such an ultimately arid experience has fascination and may provide useful insights.

But why seven stars? Fellow Shakespeareans will understand the significance of the number.[*]

> Fool: The reason why the seven stars are no more than seven is a pretty reason.
> Lear: Because they are not eight?
> Fool: Yes indeed: thou wouldst make a good fool. [33]

---

[*] The eminent astronomer, Arne Wyller, tells me that Shakespeare and his fellow writers never looked carefully at the Seven Stars (the Seven Sisters, the Pleiades), since only six are visible to the naked eye, in a cluster of more than 200.

Let there be eight discs on the desert island and ten command-ments and a hundred best tunes: I limit the first of my quests to the seven stars. Apropos of seven plays, whereas both Aeschylus and Sophocles wrote many more plays than those we have inherited, the number that has come down to us, in both cases, is seven. Were they the most popular seven, the best seven, or simply a fortuitous seven? We do not know. In Shakespeare's case, we have thirty-seven plays (thirty-eight if you include *Two Noble Kinsmen*, which I do not, simply because Heminges and Condell did not). Any attempt to limit Shakespeare to seven means we are effectively eliminating about 80 per cent of his output. What idiocy! Yet the act of choosing will help us define and better understand his greatness. The agony of having to leave out wonderful plays simply reinforces the significance of his entire output.

The plays ranked in order

Here, then, is the list of all Shakespeare's thirty-seven plays in descending order of popularity, as determined from the RSC's own attendance figures:

1. TWELFTH NIGHT
2. MACBETH
3. ROMEO AND JULIET
4. THE MERCHANT OF VENICE
5. HAMLET
6. A MIDSUMMER NIGHT'S DREAM
7. MUCH ADO ABOUT NOTHING

} **The Seven Stars**

8. THE TAMING OF THE SHREW
9. ANTONY AND CLEOPATRA
10. OTHELLO
11. THE WINTER'S TALE
12. KING LEAR
13. AS YOU LIKE IT
14. THE COMEDY OF ERRORS
15. JULIUS CAESAR
16. THE TEMPEST
17. RICHARD II
18. RICHARD III
19. HENRY V
20. THE MERRY WIVES OF WINDSOR
21. CYMBELINE
22. HENRY IV, PART I
23. MEASURE FOR MEASURE
24. HENRY IV, PART II
25. LOVE'S LABOUR'S LOST
26. CORIOLANUS
27. TROILUS AND CRESSIDA
28. ALL'S WELL THAT ENDS WELL
29. HENRY VIII
30. HENRY VI, PART I
31. HENRY VI, PART II
32. HENRY VI, PART III
33. PERICLES
34. TWO GENTLEMEN OF VERONA
35. TIMON OF ATHENS
36. KING JOHN
37. TITUS ANDRONICUS

A similar exercise for, say, 1995–2025 would be useful to update the relative popularity of the plays.

The Shakespeare Pack

I subsequently used this research in a book which I called *The Shakespeare Pack*. In the sections on each play I outlined what I consider the three main cruxes to be addressed by actors and directors, inviting them to solve the cruxes by themselves. Also, as part of the pack, I developed two sets of cards, one set designed to define requirements for mounting a production of the play such as cast numbers, playing time, sets etc; the second set suggesting appropriate quotations to learn for a fuller understanding of Shakespeare's views on the world, the individual and the imagination. The quotation pack was to be supplemented by a CD with a recording by professional actors of the quotations.

I should mention the marvellous illustrations by Clive Francis, the distinguished actor and caricaturist, that illustrate this book.

A few draft Packs were produced but these were bulky and did not convince any of the few publishers I approached to carry this project forward.

First ACT Shakespeare

However, I did finally publish a book based on the Seven Stars research and using much of the material from *The Shakespeare Pack*. I called it *First ACT Shakespeare*, a title I had already used for a programme for schools to encourage enthusiasm in children beginning Shakespeare at school and to show them how Shakespeare relates to them in the 21st century.

There's a double meaning in the words *First Act*. They define the first involvement of a child with Shakespeare, but, far more importantly, they stress that the best way to appreciate Shakespeare is to:

First, ACT Shakespeare.

and, specifically:

ACT Shakespeare rather than see Shakespeare.
SEE Shakespeare rather than read Shakespeare.
READ Shakespeare rather than ignore Shakespeare.
USE your imagination.
LEARN as much as you can by heart while you are young.

I revised *The Shakespeare Pack* specifically for young and keen Shakespearians under the title *First ACT Shakespeare*, which I published in 2021. Clive Francis produced more illustrations and Sam Carter of Tandem Publishing wrote this flyer for the book:

First ACT Shakespeare is a book about the bard – but one like no other. It is aimed primarily at young and keen Shakespeareans, students grappling with Shakespeare at school, or those about to set off to drama school.

There is a wealth of information within:

- concise summaries of the 37 plays, with three dramatic cruxes to be considered and solved before preparing any performance or production.

- a Shakespeare sampler presenting key quotations, ideal for learning by heart. These are not the usual suspects, but rather glittering examples of Shakespeare's own thoughts on the world, politics, theatre, death…

- play pages and tables with essential facts and rankings: length, balance of roles, degrees of difficulty, number of sets…

- comments on the ever-vexed authorship question.

The book is splendidly illustrated – by Clive Francis – with great Shakespearean performances, and has a foreword from Ian McKellen, followed by two important tributes.

"Here is a guide to any of us planning to embark on a Shakespeare voyage … practical and illuminating in every chapter. As you read them all, you will want to discover those plays you don't yet know. If you are further encouraged to be involved in bringing one of them to life onstage, Robert's scholarship and imagination will have been rewarded. Happy reading, happy acting and happy theatre-going." *Ian McKellen, actor*

"Robert Pennant Jones has an astonishing grasp of Shakespeare's plays. No-one else I have ever worked with – or read – has illuminated the function of every character and every action at a personal, political and philosophical level, as Jones does. It's all so vivid and graspable – yet profound. This book should be in every school in the land. I wish I'd had it at some of my rehearsals." *Robert Gillespie, theatre director*

"As a lifelong lover of Shakespeare, proud of having passed that on to some generations of schoolboys and girls in England and abroad, on stage as well as in the classroom, I was delighted by the original approach to be found in Robert Pennant Jones's excellent book, with its witty and appropriate illustrations to raise a smile." *Alan Locke, teacher*

Perdita, Antigonus, *The Winter's Tale*

This seems a good place to add some more insights into Shakespeare, some of which appear in the book.

Included in *First ACT Shakespeare* is a paragraph on 'Exit Pursued by a Bear' from *The Winter's Tale*. I would like to include an expanded account here of one of the most misunderstood stage directions in Shakespeare.

I once broadcast for the BBC World Service a short series of defining moments in Shakespeare under the title *Exit pursued by a Bear*, the famous stage direction in *The Winter's Tale*. When I directed this play I felt I learned from staging the scene that, far from being the most ridiculous and laughable stage direction in the whole canon, it is in fact one of the most profound. In this scene the old Antigonus, who has sworn an oath, has undertaken to take Leontes' and Hermione's infant child to

> Some remote and desert place…
> and that there thou leave it,
> Without more mercy, to its own protection
> And favour of the climate.

Antigonus is aware, when he lands in such a place, that it is

> Famous for the creatures of prey that keep upon't.

and he carries out his sworn duty to leave the baby, with this benediction

> Blossom, speed thee well! [35]

This is the moment of the stage direction.

The bear enters just as Antigonus is making to return to the boat that has brought him to the place. The hungry bear makes for the infant. Antigonus realises that the baby is in danger and slowly draws the bear away from the child, offering himself, sacrificing himself, as he distracts it by running away. He is exiting; and he is being pursued by the bear.

Old age has sacrificed itself for youth. A few moments later an old shepherd enters and notes to his young son who has just witnessed the death of Antigonus:

> Thou mettest with things dying, I with things
> new born. (36)

The infant Perdita is now free to achieve her destiny, and resolve the story of winter, first at the sheep shearing festival and finally at the court of Leontes. The often derided stage direction is in fact the crux of the play. And by playing the scene slowly I believe I discovered its truth.

My insight into 'Exit pursued by a Bear' prompts me to add a few other insights I learned, such as Shakespeare's anticipation of modern theatre lighting, for example.

The Stage Darkens

The actor holding Macbeth's torch in the scene where Macbeth meets Banquo and Fleance, on the battlements before Duncan's murder, thought he had but an insignificant role in that scene. Not a bit of it – there are no insignificant roles in Shakespeare. He was pleased to realise that his exit with the torch leaves the stage in imaginary darkness as his exit prepares us for

> Is this a dagger which I see before me?

In a similar way Shakespeare understood what would now be

106

called a slow fade of lighting to heighten a scene. Bottom in *A Midsummer Night's Dream* is playing the dying Pyramus. He calls on our imagination. The actor playing Moonshine is providing light for Pyramus as he stabs himself. Pyramus, expiring, utters his last:

> Now am I dead,
> Now am I fled:
> My soul is in the sky:
> Tongue, lose thy light!
> Moon, take thy flight!

At which point Moonshine exits slowly, the light thereby fading to imagined darkness and Pyramus completes his line

> Now Die, Die, Die, Die, Die. [37]

A perfect dying fall with what is in effect a slow imagined blackout.

And finally my take on the authorship question, which was also included in *First ACT Shakespeare*.

The Authorship Question

Though hardly original, my stance on the authorship question has always been:

The author was a man of the theatre.

In the canon are three plays within plays; and there are a great number of references elsewhere to acting both in the theatre and in a wider human context:

> After a well–graced actor leaves the stage [38]

> Life's but a walking shadow, a poor player that struts and frets his hour upon the stage [39]

> The baseless fabric of this vision … the great Globe itself [40]

> Speak the speech, I pray you as I pronounced it to you, trippingly on the tongue [41]

Ben Jonson's encomium is unequivocal:

> Soul of the age,
> The applause, delight, the wonder of our stage
> My Shakespeare, Rise!

And to tie the name to the man, a few lines later:

> Sweet swan of Avon… [42]

Shakespeare was named as author of the First Folio, had a bust and memorial placed in his church, had been accepted as a gentleman by award of arms, made enough money out of his theatrical career to buy property, received encomiums from other theatre figures, including Heminges and Condell.

The idea that his contemporary Christopher Marlowe was not killed in Deptford but lived on anonymously writing the plays under a pseudonym is refuted by Jonson who, while praising Shakespeare's style, specifically compares it to a different style: Marlowe's 'mighty line'. I believe that parts of *Henry VI Part I* show signs of Marlowe's collaboration with Shakespeare at an early stage of their careers, but there are two voices at work, not one.

1. Jimmy Jack and Hugh, *Translations*

2. Ellie and Shotover, *Heartbreak House*

3. Serebryakov and Yelena, *Uncle Vanya*

4. Pozzo and Estragon, *Waiting for Godot*; 5. Prospero, *The Tempest*

6. Gloucester and Lear, *King Lear*

7. Goneril and Lear, *King Lear*

8. Nell and Nagg, *Endgame*

9. Winnie, *Happy Days*

10. Opposite: Cyprus and the six locations of the play *Fathers and Daughters*, an adaptation of *Pericles*. (This and subsequent illustrations by Paul Birkbeck.)

EPHESUS

TARSUS

ANTIOCH

MYTILENE

PENTAPOLIS

TYRE

Contending gods of *Fathers and Daughters*: Neptune (11) and Diana (12).

The symbols carried by the knights in the tournament scene of *Pericles*.

13. A black Ethiope reaching at the sun.

14. Below left: A Burning Torch that's turned upside down.

15. Below right: A Wreath of Chivalry.

16. Armed Knight
Conquered by
a Lady.

17. Below left: A
Hand environ'd
with Clouds
holding out Gold
that's by the
touchstone tried.

18. Below right:
A Withered
Branch that's only
Green at Top.

Star IV

The Genius of
Christopher Marlowe

My involvement with Christopher Marlowe culminated in my devising an ambitious presentation for the Rose Theatre Trust, which I later produced under the title 'The Genius of Christopher Marlowe'.

This project came about after an invitation from Bill Dudley, the stage designer. He had conceived an exhibition at the Rose, still running, showing the outline of the original stage and auditorium; it includes a video narrated by Ian McKellen, with a brief message from Laurence Olivier, recorded days before his death.

Bill asked me to suggest a theme for a show using his computer-generated design approach. This promised to present actors as if on the stage of the Rose Theatre performing lines in the very place they were first heard. This seemed a worthwhile venture. A chance introduction through a mutual friend led me to the film and theatre director Paul Marcus, who responded to the idea and the offer to direct with huge enthusiasm. And we chose Christopher Marlowe since he too, as well as Shakespeare, had his early plays performed there. Christopher Marlowe's reputation as a playwright is not as high as it might be; his early death and the subsequent success of his great contemporary has inevitably influenced this.

The primary motivation behind this project was to raise support and money for the Rose Theatre Trust in preserving this most important theatrical site.

This was a project built on the goodwill of the actors (many of whom had already been prominent in 1989 in helping to save the site from the bulldozers), the creative team and suppliers to celebrate the genius of Christopher Marlowe.

In this spirit the actors of this show gave their services to underline the importance of the Rose Theatre in the evolution of theatre in England and the world. The key creative team offered their services in the same spirit.

The actors represented the cream of contemporary classical theatre:

Frances Barber, Samuel Barnett, Michael Burrell, Charlie Cox, Judi Dench, Joseph Fiennes, Clive Francis, Henry Goodman, Derek Jacobi, Anton Lesser, Ian McKellen, Kevin McNally, Tobias Menzies, Luke Newbury, Rebecca Night, Shaun Parkes, Alan Rickman, Antony Sher, John Shrapnel, Harriet Walter.

It is arguable that Christopher Marlowe, by the time of his death, had achieved as much as Shakespeare.

His own line on the death of Faustus:

Cut is the branch that might have grown full straight [43]

is often used as his own epitaph. I prefer to think of his life as an astonishing achievement never mind what might have been. He deserves the accolade of genius.

In devising the show I wanted to pick out four defining aspects of Marlowe's genius, namely:

Lyrical Eroticism

Marlowe was a supreme lyrical poet. While there is no evidence that Marlowe himself was gay, there is no doubt in *Edward II* and elsewhere that he beautifully expresses the idea of homosexual yearning. In *Hero and Leander* the yearning of Hero for Leander can be seen as much as a homosexual yearning as a heterosexual one. And *The Passionate Shepherd to His Love* is surely a supreme example of the young love of a boy and a girl. There is no doubt that Marlowe understood both kinds of love.

This raises the matter of boy actors in girls' roles which was the norm for Elizabethan theatre. In our times, of course, all the great female roles are played by women and we are fortunate to have top female talent to play these parts. I am in no doubt that Marlowe would have approved of having actresses rather than boys to play his female characters.

Political Daring

Marlowe's political daring is, in an Elizabethan context, straightforward. As an accredited secret service agent he understood Elizabethan realpolitik well enough. The dominant political philosophy of the age has been expounded best by Niccolo Machiavelli, the murderous Machiavel [44] in his book *The Prince*, in which expediency is the governing principle of politics. Machiavel himself appears as prologue to *The Jew of Malta*.

Success in war is seen as a definition of honour and nobility where today we may prefer diplomacy to war. The events in three of his plays were contemporary (*Massacre at Paris*) or of comparatively recent memory (*Tamburlaine*) and the events of *Edward II*'s reign were familiar history. In *Tamburlaine* in particular, victory in war and successful rebellion were seen as matters for praise. But he puts the case against war, and most eloquently too, in the Virgin's speech.

Tamburlaine's own son rejects war too, as a matter of personal rebellion against his father.

> I know, sir, what it is to kill a man;
> It works remorse of conscience in me.
> I take no pleasure to be murderous,
> Nor care for blood when wine will quench my thirst. [45]

Where Marlowe showed daring was in his treatment of the theme of deposing the lawful King, dangerous in Elizabeth's reign, though the events of Edward II's reign were more distant than the similar subject matter of Richard II, that proved rather more dangerous to Shakespeare at the time of the Essex rebellion.

Religious Daring

Accused of atheism during his life, Marlowe attacked conventional religious thinking, a very daring stance to adopt for the time.

Doctor Faustus is the play where his religious daring is most marked, the idea of selling one's soul for temporal power being a complete rejection of the idea of Christian salvation.

Marlowe is even-handed when he treats the Christianity v Islam wars in *Tamburlaine*; the Christians are punished for their perfidy and Mahomet punishes Tamburlaine for his blasphemy.

Perhaps his ability to present these ideas so succinctly and so dramatically suggests Marlowe's personal atheism. Or not.

Personal Daring

Marlowe was called "The Over-reacher" by the critic Harry Levin and many of his characters share the same characteristic: a personal daring, even a recklessness for the consequences of their actions against the established conventions of the day.

Finally we would note our debt to Marlowe in the matter of dramatic daring, what we might call today special effects. While he was a dramatist who relied primarily on the power of words rather than stage effects, the convention of the changing colours of Tamburlaine's tents can be suggested as an example of Marlowe's stage-craft. Others from *Tamburlaine* include the shooting to death by arrows of the Governor of Babylon and the entry of Tamburlaine's chariot dragged in by conquered kings. Zabina's death speech is in a theatrical style that is years before its time.

I could hardly have wished for a more distinguished cast to demonstrate the genius of Christopher Marlowe, and the programme printed their contributions in full. Here is a sample of those lines, some of which I perform via the QR codes.

This was the programme.

Spoken by Judi Dench and Derek Jacobi, from
Tamburlaine The Great, Part I

Tamburlaine, the shepherd who has conquered his way to the imperial crowns of Persia and Turkey, slaughters the Virgins of Damascus despite their pleas for mercy. Yet at such a time his thoughts turn to the possibility of attaining perfection in poetry, an impossibility he suggests, even as he utters perfect words to define it.

> What is beauty, saith my sufferings, then?
> If all the pens that ever poets held
> Had fed the feeling of their masters' thoughts,
> And every sweetness that inspir'd their hearts,

Their minds, and muses on admired themes;
If all the heavenly quintessence they still
From their immortal flowers of poesy,
Wherein, as in a mirror, we perceive
The highest reaches of a human wit;
If these had made one poem's period,
And all combin'd in beauty's worthiness,
Yet should there hover in their restless heads
One thought, one grace, one wonder, at the least,
Which into words no virtue can digest. (QR42)

Spoken by Judi Dench, from *Hero And Leander*

The poem *Hero and Leander* was unfinished at Marlowe's death and was his last major work. The beautiful Leander is described by the poet.

I could tell ye,
How smooth his breast was, and how white his belly;
And whose immortal fingers did imprint
That heavenly path with many a curious dint
That runs along his back; but my rude pen
Can hardly blazon forth the loves of men,
Much less of powerful gods.

This reminds us of Marlowe's supreme lyrical skill and reminds us of the eroticism and sexual ambivalence in his plays.

Performed by Anton Lesser, *Doctor Faustus*

Dr Faustus, having bargained with Lucifer to enjoy all earthly powers and pleasures, at the cost of his soul, commands

Mephistophilis, Lucifer's agent, to produce Helen of Troy "that I may have unto my paramour".

> Was this the face that launch'd a thousand ships,
> And burnt the topless towers of Ilium?
> Sweet Helen, make me immortal with a kiss. –

Performed by Frances Barber, from *Dido Queen of Carthage*

Aeneas, Prince of Troy, and brother-in-law of Helen, has escaped the fall of Troy and has arrived at Carthage where Dido, Queen of Carthage, becomes enraptured with him.

> I'll make me bracelets of his golden hair,
> His glistering eyes shall be my looking glass,
> His lips an altar, where I'll offer up
> As many kisses as the Sea hath sands,

Performed by Shaun Parkes as Young Spenser in *Edward II*

Young Spenser is an ambitious nobleman of the King's Party in *Edward II*. He advises the scholar, Baldock, how to prosper in dangerous times by choosing the right faction to support.

> You must be proud, bold, pleasant, resolute,
> And now and then stab, as occasion serves.

Marlowe himself later joined what we would now call the secret service under Walsingham, the Queen's spymaster. Marlowe was himself fatally stabbed at a meeting with Walsingham's agents.

Spoken by Derek Jacobi as Gaveston in *Edward II*

Gaveston, the favourite of King Edward II, plans to ingratiate himself further into the King's favour by indulging the King in wanton shows.

> Sometime a lovely boy in Dian's shape,
> With hair that gilds the water as it glides,
> Crownets of pearl about his naked arms,
> And in his sportful hands an olive-tree,
> To hide those parts which men delight to see,
> Shall bathe him in a spring;

Marlowe makes little distinction between the allure of a beautiful boy or a beautiful young woman.

Performed by Joseph Fiennes as Edward II

King Edward has been defeated by forces led by the Earl of Mortimer, who has a liaison with Isabella, Edward's Queen. He is seen here under house arrest. He is to be deposed and killed by Lightborn ('Lightborn' being the English translation of the Latin name for *Lucifer*) in appalling circumstances.

> But what are kings, when regiment is gone,
> But perfect shadows in a sunshine day?

The deposing of Kings is a dangerous theme for playwrights in Tudor times, especially at the time of the Essex rebellion.

Performed by Alan Rickman as The Duke of Guise in
The Massacre at Paris

The Duke of Guise, the persecutor of the Protestants in France, a contemporary of Marlowe's audience, spells out his ambition and methods to fulfil it in a masterpiece of Machiavellian thought.

> Now Guise, begin those deep engendered thoughts
> To burst abroad, those never dying flames
> Which cannot be extinguished but by blood.
> Oft have I levelled, and at last have learned,
> That peril is the chiefest way to happiness,
> And resolution honour's fairest aim.

For a Protestant Tudor audience Guise is the complete villain who uses religion to justify his worldly ambition.

Performed by Kevin McNally as the Prologue to
The Jew of Malta

Machiavel denigrates religion as he introduces Barabas, the Jew of Malta.

> Albeit the world think Machiavel is dead,
> Yet was his soul but flown beyond the Alps;
> …
> I count religion but a childish toy,
> And hold there is no sin but ignorance.

Performed by Henry Goodman as the Jew of Malta

The Jew of Malta defines capitalism, the rewarding of the rich by wealth, achieved by financing ventures, exploiting resources and taking risk while exposing others to the risks of wind and sea. Barabas's own capitalism includes usury too.

> Who hateth me but for my happiness?
> Or who is honour'd now but for his wealth?
> Rather had I, a Jew, be hated thus,
> Than pitied in a Christian poverty;
> For I can see no fruits in all their faith,
> But malice, falsehood, and excessive pride,

Performed by Charlie Cox and Samuel Barnett in
Tamburlaine the Great Part II

Tamburlaine's eldest son, Calyphas, deliberately ignores his father's philosophy, preferring to play cards with his companion than go to war.

> CALYPHAS
> I know, sir, what it is to kill a man;
> It works remorse of conscience in me.
> I take no pleasure to be murderous,
> Nor care for blood when wine will quench my thirst.
> …
> They say I am a coward, Perdicas, and I fear as little
> their taratantaras, their swords, or their cannons as I
> do a naked lady in a net of gold, and, for fear I should
> be afraid, would put it off and come to bed with me.

Calyphas is sure to be killed by his father for his pacifism if not hedonism.

Performed by Michael Burrell as Mycetes in
Tamburlaine the Great Part I

Mycetes, King of Persia, is about to become the first notable casualty of Tamburlaine's ambition.

> Accurs'd be he that first invented war!

Performed by Rebecca Night in *Tamburlaine the Great Part I*

After the conquest of Damascus a Virgin is deputed to plead for mercy from Tamburlaine.

> Pity our plights! O, pity poor Damascus!
> Pity old age, within whose silver hairs
> Honour and reverence evermore have reign'd!
> Pity the marriage-bed, where many a lord.
> In prime and glory of his loving joy,
> Embraceth now with tears of ruth and blood
> The jealous body of his fearful wife,

Performed by Antony Sher in *Tamburlaine the Great Part I*

Tamburlaine has defeated the Turkish Emperor Bajazeth, who becomes his footstool as he ascends Bajazeth's throne. Bajazeth and his empress are due to suffer more humiliation before their deaths.

> Now clear the triple region of the air,
> And let the Majesty of Heaven behold
> Their scourge and terror tread on emperors.

The speech is a fine example of Marlowe's 'mighty line,' and Tamburlaine is the character that most uses it, a heady mixture of vaulting ambition described in 'high astounding terms'.

Performed by Harriet Walter in *Tamburlaine the Great Part I*

Zabina, Empress of Turkey, has been captured by Tamburlaine along with Bajazeth her husband. She finds Bajazeth, having beaten out his brains against his cage.

> What do mine eyes behold? My husband dead!
> His skull all riven in twain! His brains dash'd out,
> The brains of Bajazeth, my lord and sovereign!
> O Bajazeth, my husband and my lord!
> O Bajazeth! O Turk! O Emperor!
> Give him his liquor? Not I. Bring milk and fire, and
> my blood I bring him again. – Tear me in pieces
> – give me the sword with a ball of wild-fire upon it. –
> Down with him! Down with him! – Go to my child;
> away, away, away! Ah, save that infant! Save him, save
> him! – I, even I, speak to her. – The sun was down –
> streamers white, red, black. – Here, here, here! – Fling
> the meat in his face – Tamburlaine, Tamburlaine!
> – Let the soldiers be buried. – Hell, death,
> Tamburlaine, hell! – Make ready my coach, my chair,
> my jewels. – I come, I come, I come!

Zabina's lament is extraordinary in its intense realism, quite different from anything else in the play, and prefiguring John Webster's images of death.

Performed by Anton Lesser as Faustus and Tobias Menzies as Mephistophilis in *Doctor Faustus*

Dr Faustus has powers to conjure spirits, and summons Mephistophilis. He demands to know of Lucifer, the fallen Angel, whose servant Mephistophilis is.

FAUSTUS
Tell me what is that Lucifer thy lord?

MEPHISTOPHILIS
Arch-regent and commander of all spirits.

FAUSTUS
Was not that Lucifer an angel once?

MEPHISTOPHILIS
Yes, Faustus, and most dearly lov'd of God.

FAUSTUS
How comes it, then, that he is prince of devils?

MEPHISTOPHILIS
O, by aspiring pride and insolence;
For which God threw him from the face of heaven.

FAUSTUS
And what are you that live with Lucifer?

MEPHISTOPHILIS
Unhappy spirits that fell with Lucifer,
Conspir'd against our God with Lucifer,
And are for ever damn'd with Lucifer.

FAUSTUS
Where are you damn'd?

MEPHISTOPHILIS

In hell.

FAUSTUS

How comes it, then, that thou art out of hell?

MEPHISTOPHILIS

Why, this is hell, nor am I out of it:

Faustus concludes a pact with Lucifer to surrender his soul for twenty-four years of unbridled power on Earth. The twenty-four years have all but passed and Mephistophilis is to return to conduct Faustus to Hell. With but one hour to live Faustus tries to hold back Time.

Performed by Ian McKellen as Faustus in *Doctor Faustus*

Ah, Faustus,
Now hast thou but one bare hour to live.
And then thou must be damn'd perpetually!
Stand still, you ever-moving spheres of heaven,
That time may cease, and midnight never come;
…
O lente, lente currite, noctis equi!
The stars move still, time runs, the clock will strike,
The devil will come, and Faustus must be damn'd.
O, I'll leap up to my God! – Who pulls me down?
See, see, where Christ's blood streams in the firmament!
One drop would save my soul, half a drop: ah, my
    Christ!
Ah, rend not my heart for naming of my Christ!
Yet will I call on him: O, spare me, Lucifer! –
…
Curs'd be the parents that engender'd me!

No, Faustus, curse thyself, curse Lucifer
That hath depriv'd thee of the joys of heaven.
O, it strikes, it strikes! Now, body, turn to air.
Or Lucifer will bear thee quick to hell!
O soul, be chang'd into little water-drops,
And fall into the ocean, ne'er be found!
My God, my God, look not so fierce on me!
Adders and serpents, let me breathe a while!
Ugly hell, gape not! Come not, Lucifer!
I'll burn my books! – Ah, Mephistophilis!

Spoken by Judi Dench from
The Passionate Shepherd to his Love

This lovely short poem is the epitome of Marlowe's non-dramatic work.

Come live with me, and be my love;
And we will all the pleasures prove
…
And if these pleasures may thee move,
Come live with me, and be my love.
The shepherds' swains shall dance and sing
For thy delight each May-morning:
If these delights thy mind may move,
Then live with me, and be my love.

I include it to remind ourselves of Marlowe's supreme lyrical skill.

Bonawitz pinx.   Clark & Pine Sc. 1719

The Reverend
Mr. Croxall.

Star V

A Gentleman of Cambridge

I spent thirty years or more trying to identify the author of the 1743 pamphlet called *The Lady's Preceptor*. It is gentle and urbane advice to "young ladies of distinction", done with humour and understanding. The prose is superb, as this proves, the opening line of the chapter on love:

> Love is a whimsical Passion, Madam, which deprives
> those of Wit, who had it before, and inspires those with
> it, who never had any Till then. [47]

I believe I have solved the mystery of the author's identity, and have explained why he used the pseudonym of "A Gentleman of Cambridge". At a time when women were usually regarded in society either as property or whores, I believe this is significant in treating the female sex with dignity.

THE
LADY's PRECEPTOR.

OR, A

LETTER

TO A

YOUNG LADY *of* DISTINCTION

UPON

POLITENESS.

Taken from the FRENCH of the

ABBÉ *D'ANCOURT*,

And Adapted to the

RELIGION, CUSTOMS, and MANNERS

of the *ENGLISH* NATION.

By a GENTLEMAN of CAMBRIDGE.

. . . . Adorn'd
With all that Earth or Heav'n could beſtow
To make her amiable: ----- On ſhe came,
Grace was in all her Steps, Heav'n in her Eye,
In every Geſture Dignity and Love.   MILTON.

THE THIRD EDITION.

LONDON:

Printed for J. WATTS: And Sold by B. DOD at the
Bible and *Key* in *Ave-Mary-Lane* near *Stationers-Hall.*

MDCCXLV.   [Price 1 s.

I acquired a third edition (1745) of *The Lady's Preceptor* quite by chance at a book auction when I bought a copy of *The Universal Passion*, a play by James Miller, a version of *Much Ado About Nothing*, notable for the invention of a court jester called Joculo played originally by Cibber. This too had been published in pamphlet form but had subsequently been bound with the copy of *The Lady's Preceptor*, probably as a job lot by J. Watts (the printer) or B. Dod (the bookseller), in an attempt to offload old stock. *The Universal Passion* is no improvement on Shakespeare, but *The Lady's Preceptor* struck me as superb. Take this, for example, the opening lines of the chapter on Love:

Love is a whimsical Passion, Madam, which deprives those of Wit who had it before, and inspires those with it who had never any Till then. Tis an agreeable Declivity which has its Precipices and Falls; an Enchantment which flatters the Fancy, and gives a visionary Pleasure, but at the same time there is infinite Danger in being led by it. You, Madam, are young, rich and fair, and consequently have a thousand Occasions of loving and of being loved; but these very Advantages are what lay you under an indispensable Obligation to be more circumspect and reserved than others less happy in those Respects; consider that there is nothing more important in every State of Life, than to conduct yourself, with regard to our Sex; most of them take as much, nay indeed more Pleasure in being thought to gain Victories over the Fair, than in reality to do it: This is a piece of Vanity built on the Notion, that the World must imagine them to possess some irresistible Accomplishments who could vanquish the most rigid Virtue, adorn'd with Beauty and Merit at the same time; [48] (QR43)

This wonderful prose justifies an attempt to discover who the author might be; first as being worthy of Gibbon (who is not a candidate as he was only six in 1743); second, as an early example of the male sex treating young women sympathetically; and, third, as a puzzle as to why the author hid behind his anonymity when he deserves to be known, if only to posterity. I should add that the advice on Love, quoted above, is as true today as it was fresh in the 1740s, and I shall finish this chapter with its conclusion.

I set myself the task of trying to identify the Gentleman of Cambridge and this task has taken a number of years. I had been unsuccessful until I began to consider two other books.

The first, published in 1753, called *The Accomplish'd Woman*, carries the same signature as *The Lady's Preceptor* – a Gentleman of Cambridge. The second is an old English translation of part of a French original, which the Gentleman of Cambridge "accidentally" came across, and which prompted him to translate the whole. In 1656 Walter Montague translated the first part of *L'Honnête Femme*, by a M. du Bosc, described as "a Franciscan, Counsellor and Preacher in Ordinary to the King" (i.e. Louis XIV), written in 1630.

I shall argue that *The Lady's Preceptor* (1743) and *The Accomplish'd Woman* (1753) were both by the same Gentleman of Cambridge.

The Lady's Preceptor ran to three editions in 1743/5 and was reprinted ten years later at the same time as *The Accomplish'd Woman*. *The Accomplish'd Woman* carries both a footnote and an advertisement for *The Lady's Preceptor*, which is a strong argument that the same writer was responsible for both.

The Accomplish'd Woman is a translation of a French original; *The Lady's Preceptor* claims to be an English translation of a French original, but I believe may be a completely original work. It seems to me to be particularly English, not "adapted from the French." But I must justify this by considering the introductory pages to *The Lady's Preceptor* which carry three additional names to that of the Gentleman of Cambridge: Abbé d'Ancourt, Lady Augusta and J. Watts who are, respectively, the translated author, the dedicatee and the publisher.

Abbé d'Ancourt

I have not been able to trace the existence of Abbé d'Ancourt, nor any French original of *The Lady's Preceptor*. I believe that the Gentleman of Cambridge was the author, not the translator from a French original of *The Lady's Preceptor*, as, in fact, he styles himself in the signature to the Preface. In the Preface to *The Accomplish'd Woman*, however, he makes a specific distinction between himself (translator) and du Bosc (author).

There are three possible literary candidates with names the same as, or similar to D'Ancourt, none of which seem to be him.

Florent Dancourt (1661–1725)

Florent Dancourt was born into a theatrical family. He wrote over 50 plays, mostly comedies. There is no record that he wrote Precepts as well as Plays, and he was certainly not an Abbé.

There is an attribution in the British Library catalogue that the Abbé d'Ancourt "is obviously Florent" but it is spelled Dancourt not D'Ancourt. I believe this to be a false assumption based on the coincidence of names.

Nicholas Perrot d'Ablancourt (1606–1664)

Admitted to the Academy in 1637 he became Historian to Louis XIV, though a Protestant. He is described as a translator and stylist.

P. d'Ablancourt is referred to in the Preface to *The Accomplish'd Woman* as having "answered... the several attacks of the critics in those days" on the author, and the 1632 edition of *L'Honnête Femme* carries this defence under the initials P. D.

Nicholas Fremont d'Ablancourt (1625–1694)

D'Ablancourt is better known as the French ambassador to the Portuguese court. His memoirs were published in 1668. He was the author of a Dictionary of Rhymes.

Having failed to find a convincing Abbé d'Ancourt, or a place called Ancourt with an abbey, I turned to wondering why the Gentleman of Cambridge might have chosen the particular name of Abbé d'Ancourt for the fictional author. Walter Montague, the translator of *L'Honnête Femme* (1630) re-enters the picture. Walter Montague (1603?–1677) was an unusual man. He was employed by the Duke of Buckingham in secret missions to France, in which he earned the friendship of the future Queen of Charles I, Henrietta Maria, daughter of Henri IV of France, a Catholic. After a series of adventures in which he was imprisoned in the Tower and forced to depart from England, Montague became a Catholic and by the interest of the queen-dowager of France, Mary of Medici, was made abbot of Nanteuil and, later, abbot of St Martin Pontoise.

My conclusions as to Abbé d'Ancourt are:

1. The Gentleman of Cambridge had access to a copy of Walter Montague's *The Accomplish'd Woman*, as he set out to write *The Lady's Preceptor*, adopting the French original's idea of short chapters on moral issues.

2. Wishing to disguise his authorship he decided to create a fictitious French author, a Catholic churchman, whose views might be blamed for any subsequent criticism of the text.

3. He might have known that Montague was Abbé of Nanteuil, and have shuffled details of both Montague (an Abbé) and du Bosc (a Franciscan Preacher) in concocting the fiction. He might also have remembered D'Ablancourt from the Preface to *L'Honnête Femme*.

4. The Abbé d'Ancourt does not exist and *The Lady's Preceptor* is original.

Lady Augusta

The dedication of *The Lady's Preceptor* is to Her Highness the Lady Augusta, who at the time of her birth in 1737 was second in line to the throne, being the eldest child of Frederick Prince of Wales, the eldest son of King George II. This royal birth was something of a scandal at the time and Lord Hervey's account of it, which was published years later (in 1848), gives a good account of the rivalries and tensions in the Royal Court at the time. Hervey was firmly of the King's party. The King, on learning of the pregnancy of Augusta wife of Frederick, Prince of Wales, gave strict instructions that the Princess should lie in at Hampton Court. Queen Caroline had suspected that Augusta was never likely to be pregnant and that this was likely to be "a supposititious child". Despite this command, the Prince of Wales had his wife brought, at the onset of labour, to his own palace at St James's.

The child was born – in Hervey's phrase "a little rat of a girl about the bigness of a good large toothpick" and was hurried back to court.

The christening took place in Hampton Court Chapel. The Archbishop of Canterbury performed the christening, as one would expect, but the King and Queen and other dignitaries sent proxies. Frederick declined to come on the day appointed.

This birth had great importance for this was an heir to the throne at a time when the Young Pretender's claims were still in the ascendant.

The Lady Augusta was soon supplanted by her younger brother George in 1738 who became George III in 1760. The Lady Augusta married Charles of Brunswick. Her daughter, Caroline, was destined to marry George IV, making Lady Augusta both a sister of a Queen and a mother of a Queen, though never styled Queen or Princess herself.

In 1743 the Lady Augusta was 6 and hardly old enough to need precepts of any kind. *The Lady's Preceptor* is not designed as specific advice to her, but to young women of good birth in general. Advice on such topics as Going to Court and Of Appearing Often in Public Places are not appropriate to a Royal Princess. Behaviour in such public places as Assemblies, Operas and plays is more appropriate to "young ladies of distinction" than princesses. The chapter on Gaming gives excellent advice that applies to all ranks in society. But Housewifery, for example, is well outside a princess's sphere. In general the whole tenor of *The Lady's Preceptor* is not for the benefit of the Lady Augusta but for those people who might aspire to rank and distinction.

Indeed, the real dedicatee, it seems, is

> That excellent Lady your mother ... that most excellent and accomplished Princess, the wife of Frederick Prince of Wales, Augusta of Saxe Coburg.

The compliment is doubled later,

> Observe our excellent Princess with the utmost attention in whom you will find everything to imitate that is great and amiable.

As noted, the birth of the Lady Augusta had earned the indignation of the King and Queen. Hervey (who hated the Prince of Wales) had taken "pains to bring Sir Robert (Walpole) into every scheme to mortify the Prince." Anyone dependant on Walpole's support for his own career might well, in choosing to please Frederick's party, have chosen to hide behind a pseudonym.

There is another phrase in *The Lady's Preceptor* that needs comment:

> That is the business of a spiritual tutor rather than of a worldly sage as you have sometimes been pleased to stile me.

This can hardly have been a translation since the Abbé d'Ancourt, if he existed, was certainly a spiritual tutor. If this is original to *The Lady's Preceptor* it suggests that the author may not be in holy orders, which I had initially suspected. However, in coming up with a churchman as my Gentleman of Cambridge, as I shall shortly reveal, I reflected that Princess Augusta seemed to place more value on his worldliness than his spirituality.

The phrase "worldly sage" fits *The Lady's Preceptor* perfectly. Might denying being a "spiritual tutor" be a further piece of literary camouflage, like the Gentleman of Cambridge, to protect his identity from his enemies? In this regard the chapters in *The Lady's Preceptor* on spiritual matters argue at the very least that the author was determined to cover religious as well as worldly advice, but to a modest extent.

J. Watts

Both *The Lady's Preceptor* and *The Accomplish'd Woman* were published by J. Watts, and sold by B. Bod. Watts had succeeded J. Tonson as the pre-eminent figure of the day in publishing. An association with Watts would be important evidence in confirming the identity of the author.

SO, WHO IS THE GENTLEMAN OF CAMBRIDGE?

I began my search for the Gentleman of Cambridge with the following necessary conditions to be considered and met:

Age

At least forty in 1743 – a younger man would hardly have achieved the Preceptor's urbanity of style. And, since the Gentleman of Cambridge's translation of *The Accomplish'd Woman* appeared in 1753, it would suggest life starting not later than 1700, ending not before 1753.

Cambridge

A plausible Cambridge connection.

Politics

Aligned with opposition to Walpole and sympathetic to the court of Frederick Prince of Wales.

Career

A career that does not preclude writing to a professional standard.

Literary Ability

I assume that *The Lady's Preceptor* was not a unique piece of work and that the Gentleman of Cambridge had demonstrated literary ability in other writing, with a similar literary fingerprint. The literary fingerprint is a guide that compares the number of syllables/word a writer typically uses compared with other writers. A high syllables/word score denotes a prolix style (e.g. Gibbon) and a low score a simple style (e.g. Richardson). I use this measure (with others) as a help in including, or rejecting, possible candidates as author. It is useful, too, in comparing an author's different works if that author chooses to write in different styles.

Use of Nom de Plume

A record of using a nom de plume would lend considerable weight.

Connection with J. Watts

Though not essential, a record of an association with the publishing business of J. Watts would be an advantage.

As time went by I added another criterion which seemed important, particularly thinking of the chapter on Love. This is:

The Author's Treatment of Women

The Lady's Preceptor demonstrates a sympathetic attitude to the female sex, not at all usual at that time. This was an age where women were treated as property (for their money) or whores (for their favours), a time when Wycherley was still being performed and Fanny Hill due to appear. This author introduces the idea of a rounded individual that seems characteristic of women later in the century like Fanny Burney and Jane Austen, the author himself more a Sydney Smith than a Dean Swift.

The Lady's Preceptor is sympathetic to young women, especially in achieving a social acceptance when more attention was being accorded to young men. The whole tone of *The Lady's Preceptor* is of urbanity, coloured with wit and understanding, not being at all didactic, but suggestive in its precepts, recognising that perfection will never be achieved, and some falling short of perfection not to be blamed and even enjoyed. The early candidates I considered are all male-oriented in their writing.

STEP FORWARD DR CROXALL

Having got so far without revealing the author of *The Lady's Preceptor*, it is time to present him. It was only after having investigated the claims of Chesterfield, Hammond, Walpole, Bubb Doddington and Bentley that I chanced on a name which, if not actually staring me in the face, was one of the earliest in my notebook, the Reverend Samuel Croxall. R. D. Croxall's translation of Aesop's Fables is advertised in *The Lady's Preceptor* along with some other books, and the thought occurred to me that this might be a hint as to his identity.

Using his entry in the *Dictionary of National Biography* I ticked off his claims against the criteria I had chosen.

Age

Born c. 1690. Died 1752.

This makes him c. fifty-three in 1743, ideal for the worldly preceptor. His death in 1752 does not rule him out as the translator of *The Accomplish'd Woman* published in 1753 which could have been brought to publication for him by another, he having completed the translation before his death.

Education

St John's College, Cambridge. BA 1711, MA 1717.

Politics and the Royal Connection

Croxall in his young days had curried favour from the court of King George I – he had written an ode welcoming the King from Hanover in 1714. As a young cleric he preached a sermon in St Paul's in 1715 – Incendiaries no Christians – where he was described as Chaplain in Ordinary to His Majesty for the Chapel Royal at Hampton Court.

However, Croxall preached another sermon in which the Prime Minister of the day, Sir Robert Walpole, was attacked as a figure "of a corrupt and wicked Minister of State." It seems that Walpole had stood in Croxall's way over some ecclesiastical appointment he had sought. Despite this, Croxall was not relieved of his chaplaincy, being regarded by the Court as a staunch supporter of the Hanoverian Succession, and Croxall added to this support with a 1715 poem, *The Vision*, and another praising the Duke of Argyll on his victory over the Jacobite Pretender.

Unfortunately for Croxall, Walpole's long career as Prime Minister and his continuing opposition to Croxall's advancement caused Croxall to burn his boats once and for all with his 1730 Epistle to Sir Robert Walpole.

In publishing this attack on Walpole, Croxall, now aged forty, evidently had come to terms with the realisation that he would never become a bishop despite his obvious credentials. A few extracts confirm this:

> If Truth may be asked sir Pray what does it mean,
> My pretensions so fair I'm not yet a dean.
>
> That my Ovid, my Aesop, Circassian and all,
> The gay things I have wrote should not merit a stall?
>
> When the Muse has long begg'd that you always
>   should slight her,
> Who had hopes of exchanging his wreaths for a Mitre,
> By your pride or contempt My Laurel's ill fated,
> Translating so often – and never translated
> But since you were pleased to refuse my request
> Thank yourself – if I painted you none of the best
> If your person I scorn, and your counsels oppose
> And preach for the King while I write for his foes

It can hardly be said that Croxall wrote for the King's Foes – notably the Jacobites, but it may mean that he turned his support to Frederick Prince of Wales whose relations with the king were bad, in effect taking a long view on continuing pro-Hanoverian support. Walpole continued to be Croxall's nemesis until his death in 1745.

It can be inferred that Croxall's attitude to money was that of wanting plenty. His numerous ecclesiastical appointments show that he was materially well off. He earned money as an author (and as an editor too) as this final couplet shows:

> Whate'er some may fancy, the profit's the same
> If I have it in cash what is wanting in Fame.

Career

Despite not being made a bishop, Croxall made notable progress in the Church, becoming Chancellor of Hereford Cathedral in 1738 and obtaining other livings throughout his career. He became Doctor of Divinity in 1728.

So, his ecclesiastical career was successful and the numerous livings he enjoyed would have made him wealthy. Note the vicarage of Hampton – the parish which includes the Royal Palace at Hampton Court – which he held to his death.

Politics and Royal Connection

He must, therefore, have been aware of the events surrounding the birth of Lady Augusta in 1737. I believe he might well have assisted the Archbishop of Canterbury at her baptism in the Royal Chapel. Though I have not been able to establish whether Croxall was present at the baptism, it is tempting to think that he would have been there or thereabouts.

Croxall had already dedicated his contribution to Ovid's *Metamorphoses* in 1717 to Princess Anne, a sister of George II (when she was only eight). He continued to earn the favour of the Hanoverian Court, which protected him against Walpole in 1730. I find it plausible that he sought to keep favour with the court, especially the court of Frederick Prince of Wales, by dedicating *The Lady's Preceptor* to Lady Augusta (aged six) but in stricter truth to the Princess of Wales her mother.

By blood Princess Augusta was German. She was eighteen years old at the birth of Lady Augusta in a foreign country beset with enemies at court. Her mother-in-law Queen Caroline was vehemently opposed to Frederick Prince of Wales and to Lady Augusta, whom she suspected of being a foundling. Croxall was in a perfect position to advise and assist her in playing down his spiritual guidance and concentrating on more worldly matters. The advice in *The Lady's Preceptor* is apparently French, drawing on Italian authors, for the benefit of a German Princess in a hostile English environment and under attack from a Scottish Pretender. However, the superb English prose strongly suggests this is an English original.

As to opportunity, though clearly busy with church affairs at Hereford, Croxall would have visited Hampton where his father, who had been his predecessor as vicar from 1714–1716, still lived. His father died in 1739. Croxall never resigned his connections in Hampton.

Literary Ability

Croxall, while still in his twenties had been commissioned to translate several books of Ovid's *Metamorphoses*, under the editorship of Samuel Garth, with others, such as the Poet Laureate John Dryden. Croxall, still in his twenties, had clearly impressed the literary giants of the day with his ability.

Croxall's other claim to literary merit is his successful prose translations of Aesop's Fables which appeared in 1722, each with a moral commentary by him in an edition enhanced by woodcuts of each fable that helped to keep it popular well into the next century. The prose is deliberately simple – the book is designed for children.

Croxall is certainly of high literary merit.

Literary Fingerprint

The fingerprint of *The Lady's Preceptor* is 1.48 syllables per word. This compares with typical scores for Gibbon (1.58) and Johnson (1.51) at one end; and with Richardson (1.28) and Swift (1.32) at the other. Croxall's overall score is also 1.48 but this is an average of a wide range of outputs. Though Croxall's average is apparently a close fit with *The Lady's Preceptor*, it is not sufficiently close to the scores for the Fables (1.38/1.42) or Scripture Politics (1.62) to be convincing proof that he is the Gentleman of Cambridge. However, a sermon by Croxall in Hereford Cathedral on The Antiquity, Dignity and Advantages of Music preached in 1741 (i.e. contemporaneous with *The Lady's Preceptor*) scores 1.49. This is reassuring, not only that the averages for Croxall exactly match the score for *The Lady's Preceptor*, but that the score for the sermon was close enough too. Add to this the style of the sermon itself; learned, sympathetic, gentle and urbane, similar to my ears to the style of *The Lady's Preceptor*. These are persuasive arguments that Croxall is its author.

Nom de Plume

I can think of three reasons why Croxall wished to use a nom de plume. First, so as not to excite the wrath of Walpole's administration, second, to protect his ecclesiastical preferments, and third to make advances to a young lady.

He has a considerable track record of using such. Croxall's first publication (1713–14) *Cantos of Spencer* appeared under the name of Nestor Ironside. The erotic poem *The Fair Circassian* was ascribed to a Gentle Commoner of Oxford and also carried the initials R. D. In this instance his cover was blown in notorious circumstances and, as already quoted above, he acknowledged his authorship of *The Fair Circassian* in his Epistle to Sir Robert Walpole.

I note too that Croxall had hidden behind the initials R. D. as well as an Oxford identity which was doubly false for he went to Cambridge. In the case of *The Accomplish'd Woman* of 1753, he evidently sought to muddy the issue with a second falsehood by signing the preface with the initials L. M.

L. M. is a disguise I have not been able to penetrate (R. D. is unexplained too). L. M. may have made the final preparations for the publication, if Croxall was incapacitated in his last days.

What is indisputable, however, is that Croxall used different pseudonyms to conceal his authorship throughout his career. I believe a Gentleman of Cambridge is one of them.

Connection with Publisher J. Watts

Croxall was only twenty-seven when commissioned to provide some translations for Ovid's *Metamorphoses*, published by J. Tonson in 1717. Tonson retired in 1720 and died in 1726.

Croxall's poem, 'The Vision', was published by Tonson in 1715. The Fables of Aesop were published by J. Tonson and Watts in 1720, (this Jacob Tonson being the son of old Jacob Tonson who had retired). Croxall acted as editor for Watts between 1720 and 1722. The links between Watts and Croxall are evidently very strong.

Attitude to Women

As a young man Croxall was clearly attracted by young women as evidenced in his Ovid translations, and his poems *The Fair Circassian* and *Ode to Florinda* – each display a young man's delight in female beauty, even to the point of suppressed lust.

And it may be that this young man's ardour, taking into account his hopes for clerical advancement, might have persuaded him not to marry early and only to revisit the subject for "young ladies of distinction," anonymously, towards the end of his life.

Ovid's *Metamorphoses* treats of nymphs, goddesses and maidens in a variety of amatory encounters, not excluding rape.

Croxall's contributions are enthusiastic as the following show:

> Tereus beheld the virgin, and admir'd
> And with the coals of burning Lust was fired;
> Such charms in any breast might kindle Love
> But him the Heats of Inbred Lewdness move.

Each of the twelve books of the *Metamorphoses* has an engraving of dedication. Croxall's Book 6 has a picture of a bare-breasted nymph in anguish, or in ecstasy.

In *The Fair Circassian* Croxall goes further in celebrating the erotic over the spiritual. As Ovid is to classicists so is 'The Song of Solomon' to churchmen who admire women. Is there not admiration, and more, in this?

> Her even breasts like the Roe's younglings play
> And panting bound, luxuriant as they
> Like velvet buds the crimson nipples rise
> Firm to the touch and grateful to the eyes

Croxall's poem *Florinda* was written in the same vein at the same time, but published later.

> Her eyes, her lips, her breasts exactly round,
> Of Lily hue, unnumber'd arrows sent,
> Which to my heart an easy passage found,

Thrilled in my bones and thro' my Marrow went;
Some bubbling upward through the water came,
Prepar'd by Fancy, to augment my flame.

This young classicist-cleric admired the female sex and in particular one young lady. Croxall dedicated *The Fair Circassian* to Miss Anna Maria Mordaunt, the daughter of a man who had entertained him at his house. The dedication is quite explicit, and seems an elaborate marriage proposal: "To you I owe my creation, as a lover, and in the being of your beauty only I live and move and exist."

The Fair Circassian was ascribed to a Gentleman Commoner of Oxon. A supposed tutor explained that the author was a young man who subsequently died "of that distemper which physicians call a fever upon the spirit." It seems the secret soon became known. Horace Walpole mentioned in a letter that a young gentleman in Oxford wrote *The Fair Circassian* to Anna Maria Mordaunt, a maid of honour to Queen Caroline and died of love of her. Any thought Croxall may have had of a relationship with Anna Maria Mordaunt did not survive what the *Dictionary of National Biography* calls "an unpleasing notoriety to his name." And, to add comment to this affair, in *The Lady's Preceptor* is this: "To be a Maid of Honour is the readiest way to a dishonourable woman."

Croxall was not finished with the Mordaunts and he dedicated a volume of the *Select Collection of Novels* which he had edited to Miss Elizabeth Lucy Mordaunt, "probably a sister to Anna Maria." Had his motive in either case been marriage he was unsuccessful and I thought at first he did not marry as a result, since the *Dictionary of National Biography* does not mention it. However, he did marry, in 1717, an heiress, Philippa Proger. Through this marriage Croxall was able to enjoy his wife's inheritance and her family home where he took up residence from time to time. Philippa (born c. 1670) was aged about forty-seven at the time of her marriage to Croxall and as might be expected no children came of this marriage. It is evident that Croxall's reason for marriage was more to do with money and comfort than sex and excitement.

By the time he began writing *The Lady's Preceptor* Croxall was in his fifties. His wife was in her seventies and was to die in 1745. The time may have come for more mature and less passionate precepts for young ladies than his earlier juvenile ardours. He seems to have revisited his thoughts on the female sex in a style less classic than Ovid, less erotic than the 'Song of Solomon' and still agreeable to the house of Hanover.

Conclusion

A final piece of evidence that convinces me that the Gentleman of Cambridge is Dr Samuel Croxall is contained in the Preface to *The Accomplish'd Woman*: the Translator italicises his inscription to the Women of Great Britain. The footnote on page 5 of Chapter 1 in which *The Lady's Preceptor* is advertised is also in italics. And in the Preface itself are other italics, written either by the translator (or by L. M.) which I take as conclusive evidence that proclaim his identity. I note the words Fable on page 3, Metamorphosis on page 45 and Precepts on page 9. These are surely describing Croxall, for Croxall translated Aesop's Fables, some books of Ovid's *Metamorphoses* and, I argue, wrote *Precepts for Young Ladies of Distinction*.

Samuel Croxall's age, education, politics, connection with the court, career, literary ability, use of pseudonyms and connection with J. Watts the publisher, all fit the criteria I set myself. I now unmask him as the Gentleman of Cambridge, the author of *The Lady's Preceptor*, and translator of *The Accomplish'd Woman*.

I may conclude with his sympathetic treatment of women and, especially, his chapter on Love. This is as valid today as it was in the middle of the eighteenth century and I conclude with the continuation of the quotation that suggested I search for its author in the first place.

> It is therefore highly necessary for you, Madam, to avoid ever dropping an Expression that may flatter their Vanity, or give them a Glimpse of Hope that they might succeed in their Pursuit; for as they have a greater Regard for their own Reputation than for yours, they will be always ready to take more than you ought to allow them. A Woman, who is willing to go as great Lengths in their Favour as she may do without Imputation, will be mighty apt to take a little Step farther, without being much startled at it. You may have shewn a Civility perhaps, or even some slight piece of Complaisance, without thinking any thing more of the matter; but one of those presumptuous Sparks, who construes every thing agreeable to the Opinion he has of his own sweet Person, is a very dangerous Interpreter: He won't fail to persuade himself that you think as he does, and will conclude, in spite of all your Precautions, that you intend to make him happy in time. [49] (QR44)

As well as the words on love, I have recorded two other examples of Croxall's advice: on gaming (sound and sensible) and on the "choice and entertainment of books" (not entirely consistent with modern ideas of what a young lady should read). But the prose is wonderful and can be accessed via the QR codes. (QR45) (QR46)

Marina and Pericles
Pericles

Star VI

Fathers and Daughters

This was a project for a film based on Shakespeare's play *Pericles*, which I called *Fathers and Daughters*, which had a long gestation, to which I shall return. But first the development of the key ideas.

While living in New York in 1970 I co-directed a production of *Pericles* for the CSC Repertory Company, an Off Off Broadway theatre group. We had a limited number of actors and it occurred to me that the character Lysimachus, who looks to corrupt the virgin Marina in a brothel, but is won over by her virtue, is in many ways the antithesis of the young hero Pericles. It made sense in that production to double the characters of Pericles and Lysimachus, showing two sides of the "same" character, one who resists temptation, the other who may not.

This worked even if the actor had to age quickly to resume playing the old Pericles.

Much later it occurred to me that rather than ageing up a young actor to play the grief-stricken Pericles, an older actor would be preferable. It then struck me that the central theme of the play is not so much about the adventures of the eponymous hero, but rather the relationships of fathers to their daughters, one of whom is the old Pericles.

This in turn led to the idea that there were four Father/Daughter relationships and also that there were four Male and Female Guardianships, the hero having the two relationships mentioned above.

These are the four FATHER and DAUGHTER relationships:

(1) Antiochus + Antiochus's Daughter	A corrupt incestuous relationship.
(2) Simonides + Thaisa	A noble relationship, even if Simonides threatens to be ignoble at one point.
(3) Boult + Marina	A corrupt quasi-paternal relationship which threatens to end in rape and "incest".
(4) Pericles + Marina	The noblest relationship where the daughter becomes the parent. Her goodness rescues (gives life to) the father.

This means that the theme of <u>YOUNG LOVE</u> is secondary. As it happens we hardly have a chance to explore these relationships since they are finished with almost as soon as they are begun. It occurs in two modes:

(1) Pericles + Thaisa	The central (good) marriage that survives misfortune.
(2) Lysimachus + Marina	An apparently good marriage (we never find out), though the portents were not propitious when Lysimachus was about to act corruptly.

The third theme is that of <u>GUARDIANSHIP</u> in both its good and its corrupt guises. A male and a female guardian, sometimes in partnership, make up the theme in six variations:

(1) Cleon + Dionyza	Apparently good, they betray their trust.
(2) Helicanus	The touchstone of goodness.
(3) Lychorida	The good Nurse preserves the infant.

(4) Cerimon	The doctor, a just wise man.
(5) Pandar + Bawd	The brothel owners who exploit for gain, where they should protect.
(6) Diana	Goddess Argentine, protectress of Thaisa and the final Dea ex Machina.

The suggestion then is to have six main actors, five of whom switch throughout from the good to the bad sides of their natures.

It should be noted that two actors play the role of Pericles.

1. FATHER — Antiochus/Simonides/Boult/Old Pericles

2. DAUGHTER — Antiochus's Daughter/Thaisa/Marina

3. HERO — Young Pericles/Lysimachus

4. GUARDIAN — Helicanus/Cleon/Cerimon/Pandar

5. GUARDIAN — Dionyza/Lychorida/Diana/Bawd

6. STORYTELLER — Gower

What about the scenes where they appear together? Well, they hardly ever do! There are three instances where one of the alter ego characters speaks, but in each case it is a matter of but one line which could be cut, or the secondary character could be represented by a double.

The dynamic tension of the plot is the contention between two gods Neptune and Diana. [P11] [P12] Diana is the Goddess of childbirth and chastity and is the protectress of the innocent daughters, Thaisa and Marina. Neptune is angry with the hero, subjecting him to two sea storms. He relents only on the day of his feast in Mytilene, where, in the harbour, the sea now calm at last, the gentle rocking of the boat allows the daughter, Marina, to revive her father.

Note that Marina

> For I was born at sea

is never away from the sea: her birth; the seaside walk; the capture by pirates; the brothel –

> She would serve after a long voyage at sea and on board ship in the harbour.

During the time these ideas were maturing, either for a possible stage production, or, as it happened, the pilot film script of *Fathers and Daughters*, I became obsessed with the six symbols carried by the knights in the tournament scene.

These symbols are usually represented by bad and anachronistic heraldry, and in every production I have ever seen are forgotten as soon as done.

My view is that the symbols of the shields are consciously chosen and in fact replete with meaning. They should be seen like leitmotifs in music to explain and enhance the play. Each symbol represents the thesis or antithesis of one of the play's themes.

So, what are the symbols (with their respective mottos translated), and how do they fit the foregoing?

> 1. The Black Ethiope reaching at the Sun.
>   (Thy light is life to me) [P13]

and

> 2. A Burning Torch that's turned upside down.
>   (Consumed with what it was nourished by) [P14]

might be taken as comments on the Father–Daughter relationship. The child "holds his life" of the father – the sun. The sun is good; "Thy Light is life to me". The child 'reaches' to aspire to the Father. But Blackness is equivocal – in this play blackness is associated with incest. If the image of 1. is 'good' the blackness questions the goodness. Turn it upside down – the sun becomes the consuming fire that destroys, in the same way that the flame would destroy the torch if the torch were turned upside down. The hair of the daughter becomes the flame that is lit and destroys. In the 'good' case Thaisa looks to her father as the sun (one of the knights refers to Simonides as the sun). In the corrupt case Antiochus's desire reverses the natural order of things: "Beauty hath his power and wit which can as well inflame as it can kill".

There are three symbols that refer to the Lovers' relationship:

3. A Withered Branch that's only Green at Top.
(In this hope I live) [P18]

4. An Armed Knight conquered by a Lady.
(More by gentleness than by force) [P16]

5. A Wreath of Chivalry.
(Triumph leads me forth) [P15]

Young Pericles comes from the ordeal of the shipwreck and attends the tournament in Pentapolis armed only with a withered branch (blackened by fire?). But as with the tree in *Waiting for Godot*,

"Yesterday it was all black and bare, but now it's covered with leaves." [50]

The greenness is a sign of hope. He wins the tournament through force of arms (an arm'd knight, literally, for the sailors restored his armour to him). But he was won "More by gentleness than by force" by the qualities of Thaisa, and "conquered by the lady". Subsequently, the lady Marina conquers Lysimachus, her knight, by gentleness not force.

The fifth symbol picks up greenness, this time with the wreath of triumph: "The crown of triumph has led me on". Pericles thought he had won this in Pentapolis but he must wait until the end of the play before Gower restores it to him "crown'd with joy at last". This symbol has the idea of a hand (Gower's?) holding the wreath above his head.

6. A Hand environ'd with Clouds holding out Gold that's by the touchstone tried.
        (Thus faithfulness is to be tried) (P17)

The sixth symbol has a hand explicitly. It holds 'true' gold (sun?) and is the symbol of true faithfulness or, in my scheme, of good guardianship. It fits Helicanus well – lots of references – and Cerimon. "Thus is faithfulness to be tried…"; a powerful symbol for trust given and requited. Compare this with the symbols 1. and 2. for the false guardian, Cleon, who is consumed by fire.

These symbols, then, are clear echoes, leitmotifs, that can be staged representationally, or hinted by gesture or by position, or in music, or in other ways to pick up other resonances that refer to these same basic ideas of the play.

Is this all strained and fanciful? I hope not! Why should the symbols be so elaborately explained? There has to be a reason. They should surely not be hurried over or forgotten. The plays of the day were moving towards the Court Masque – a new convention. Each figure in the masque was given meaning not always clear. Divining the meaning was an intellectual challenge to the audience of the day. The riddle is a powerful convention of the period – we have already had one in this play at the court of Antiochus. The symbols seem to work as if highlighting the story. But is this just a bee in my bonnet? The culmination of the play is Gower's last speech (the last speech in the Folio!). [QR47] The following chart shows how I think the six symbols are represented in that speech.

BLACK ETHIOPE BURNING TORCH	In Antiochus and his daughter, you have heard of monstrous lust the due and just reward.	ANTIOCHUS and DAUGHTER
WITHERED BRANCH	In Pericles, his Queen, and daughter seen – Although assail'd with fortune fierce and keen –	HERO THAISA MARINA
ARMED KNIGHT	Virtue preserv'd from fell destructions blast.	
WREATH OF CHIVALRY	Led on by heaven, and crown'd with joy at last.	GOWER
A HAND … HOLDING GOLD	In Helicanus you may well descry A figure of truth, of faith, of loyalty. In Reverend Cerimon there well appears The worth that learned charity aye wears.	HELICANUS CERIMON
BURNING TORCH	For wicked Cleon and his wife, when fame.	CLEON AND DIONYZA

BURNING TORCH	Had spread their cursed deed, and honour'd name of Pericles, to rage the city turn	
	That him and his they in his palace burn:	
	The gods for murder seemed so content	DIANA
	To punish them; although not done, but meant.	NEPTUNE
	So on your patience evermore attending	GOWER
	New joy wait on you!	
	Here our play hath ending.	SHAKESPEARE

I began to develop the film script for *Fathers and Daughters* around the millennium and spent some time in Cyprus, a perfect location where all six settings of the play could be convincingly filmed. [P10] As I sought to interest possible backers I wrote this introduction to the script:

FATHERS AND DAUGHTERS

A screenplay based on *Pericles* by William Shakespeare.

- An ancient storyteller comes from the past to tell the stories.

- Four fathers and their daughters. Four relationships – some virtuous, some vicious. A hero challenges the fathers for their daughters.

- The God Neptune is angry with the hero. Neptune contends with the Goddess Diana who strives to protect the daughters.

- Guardians sometimes protect and sometimes exploit the daughter and the hero. The action takes place in six locations around the Mediterranean.

The four stories of *Fathers and Daughters* are:

INCEST

The hero discovers the vicious father's incest with his daughter and flees the father's rage. The dominant element is FIRE.*

JOINING

The wise father joins his daughter with the virtuous hero. The dominant element is AIR.*

PROSTITUTION

The virtuous daughter wins over the father who would prostitute her in a brothel. The hero is also converted by the daughter. The dominant element is EARTH.*

JOYS

The daughter gives new life to her father who experiences a sea of joys after great sorrows; and is betrothed to the hero. The dominant element is WATER.*

* The four elements are all mentioned in Pericles' line to his newborn daughter in the storm:

> As childing a nativity as fire, air, water, earth and heaven can make.

There is also:

- a deadly riddle
- a storm at sea and a shipwreck
- a quarterstaff tournament with tableaux vivants of naked boys and girls
- a sexy dance
- a childbirth at sea
- Neptune v. Diana
- a sea walk and some pirates
- a brothel in crisis
- and … the gentle rocking of a boat in a harbour where strange truths are revealed.

At Ephesus, in Diana's temple, virtue is triumphant in a fabulous resolution to these themes. The ancient storyteller reveals to us he is Shakespeare.

I made an eighty-minute pilot version of the script to show the potential of the multi-part actors: John McEnery, Vanessa Earl, Alun Raglan, Frances Barber and Alan David.

Paul Birkbeck, an artist friend, created the six symbols for Gower's book. There were also a map of the six locations surrounding Cyprus, and portraits of the contending gods, and illustrations of other key scenes. Though prepared for the film version of the play, so far unmade, these remain valid, I suggest, as comment on the text, and many of these are illustrated in plates five to eight.

Little Gidding

Star VII

Four Quartets

The great actor Paul Scofield failed, as far as I was concerned, to make T. S. Eliot's *Four Quartets* sufficiently clear, or of enough variety, in his reading for radio of the poems, shortly before he died. And Ralph Fiennes's recent performance, though superbly articulated and imaginatively performed, suffered, in my view, from the same lack of textual variety. Rather than rely on one distinguished voice for the reading, I prepared a four-voice version. The title of the poems suggests four-ness and I identified these quite distinct strands in each of the four poems.

The four contrasting voices are of a boy; a young man; an experienced man and an old man. This range of ages suggests their corresponding four seasons: the boy spring, the young man summer, the experienced man autumn and the old man winter, though midwinter is also linked with spring in the opening words of the last of the quartets, 'Little Gidding'. As well as having four different locations, the four elements are the fourth of the distinctive strands which seem to fit the poems: air for 'Burnt Norton', earth for 'East Coker', water for 'The Dry Salvages' and fire finally to be linked with the rose at the conclusion of 'Little Gidding'. These are summarised here.

Location	Dominant Element	Dominant Season	Dominant Voice
Burnt Norton	Air	Spring	Old Man/Boy
East Coker	Earth	Summer	Young Man
The Dry Salvages	Water	Autumn	Experienced Man
Little Gidding	Fire	Midwinter	Old Man

So a four-voice version of *Four Quartets* may offer the listener more variety, more suggestion and more meaning than even the most skilful single voice. The four voices open 'Burnt Norton' and this, with the last section from 'Little Gidding', can be heard via the QR codes. [QR48] [QR49] What do you think of this treatment?

I was pleased with the result and, maybe, this is a significant original contribution for a future edition, either of the poems themselves or for performance.

"Speak the speech, I pray you as I pronounced it to you…"
Hamlet

SOME QUOTATIONS FOR LIFE

Infinite Riches in a Little Room [(51)]

Great writing has helped me to define and understand some of the great themes of life, namely the imagination; precepts for living; and the realities of time, from birth to death.

This chapter's heading is a line from Marlowe's play *The Jew of Malta*, which Barabas uses to describe the contents of a jewel case. I use it to describe a significant distillation of wisdom in a small space, often a few lines of poetry. Attention spans nowadays are shorter than they were, even at the beginning of my lifetime, so compressions of thought and meaning into a little space are fit for a new generation.

I have always preferred plays to novels insofar as the dramatist compresses into two or three hours what a novelist takes many more to deliver. Samuel Beckett's plays vividly demonstrate this compression of thought and, indeed, movement. From normal movement in *Waiting for Godot*, Beckett gradually diminishes the movement of his characters. In *Endgame* three of the four characters are confined to urns or a wheelchair. In *Play* all three characters are in urns. In *Happy Days* the main character Winnie is virtually immobile up to her waist in sand, and in the second half she is completely immobile but for her head. And in *Not I* the only actor is reduced to a mouth. This compression forces us to concentrate on the words, on what is said rather than what is seen. And in *Lessness*, which takes the compression of words even further, this wonderful phrase, which stands out against the bleakness of the other lines, defines both the imagination and poetry itself.

In an earlier chapter I mentioned the millennial advertisement I took out for my granddaughters in the *International Herald Tribune*. These are included here and marked with an asterisk.

* Never but imagined

the blue

in a wild imagining

The blue celeste of poesy [(52)]

In his play *Tamburlaine the Great*, Christopher Marlowe describes the rise and eventual fall of one who would conquer the world. At one point he wrestles with the dilemma of whether to conquer Egypt, the home of his wife Zenocrate's father. For a moment he abandons thoughts of conquest to thoughts of immortal poesy, which I quoted earlier, but are well worth repeating here:

> If all the pens that ever poets held
> Had fed the feeling of their masters' thoughts,
> And every sweetness that inspir'd their hearts,
> Their minds, and muses on admired themes;
> If all the heavenly quintessence they still
> From their immortal flowers of poesy,
> Wherein, as in a mirror, we perceive
> The highest reaches of a human wit;
> If these had made one poem's period,
> And all combin'd in beauty's worthiness,
> Yet should there hover in their restless heads
> One thought, one grace, one wonder, at the least,
> Which into words no virtue can digest. [(53)] [(QR50)]

This seems to me extraordinary, that a warrior should interrupt his quest to conquer by defining poetry in this way, and defining its ultimate inability to achieve an absolute perfection. For me, however, this is an ultimate perfection, an example of

* Infinite riches in a little room. [51]

Shakespeare sometimes interrupts plots to define his art. *Hamlet,* already long, is interrupted by Hamlet's advice to the players, as to how his plays are to be performed: it is of course Shakespeare speaking, not the prince. In *A Midsummer Night's Dream* Theseus interrupts the story, defining theatrical imagination:

* And, as imagination bodies forth
The forms of things unknown, the poet's pen
Turns them to shapes, and gives to airy nothing
A local habitation and a name.

Theseus also excuses indifferent performance of his author's play:

* The best in this kind are but shadows,
And the worst are no worse
if imagination amend them.

The foregoing quotations have a theatrical context and some can provide precepts for life. In *A Midsummer Night's Dream* Bottom the weaver, and would-be actor, gives his colleagues this envoi at the end of the first rehearsal for the play they are to perform before the Duke Theseus:

* Take pains; be perfect; adieu.

For actors the exhortation *be perfect* simply means learn your lines. But for mankind in general perfection is an aspiration hardly ever achieved, but God may help us to approach it. And, for both the actor and mankind, taking pains is the only way to achieve perfection. This five-word precept is *infinite riches* indeed.

On a more worldly scale, wise advice is given in *Hamlet* by Polonius to his son:

> This above all: to thy own self be true,
> And it must follow, as the night the day,
> Thou canst not then be false to any man.

These precepts cannot escape the verdict of

> That old common arbitrator, Time. [54]

And we must ultimately accept that

> For beauty, wit,
> high birth, vigour of bone, desert in service,
> Love, friendship, charity, are subjects all
> to envious and calumniating Time. [64]

This reality introduces sleep and dreams. As Hamlet has it

> O God, I could be bounded in a nutshell,
> and count myself a king of infinite space,
> were it not that I have bad dreams. [55]

My own belief, not Hamlet's, is that our little life is rounded with a sleep. [56] As the troubled King Henry IV puts it:

O Sleep! O Gentle sleep,
Nature's soft nurse, how have I frighted thee
that thou no more wilt weigh mine eyelids down
and steep my senses in forgetfulness? (56)

For me the greatest hope is that death ends all, and is the supreme benefit of forgetfulness. As Vladimir puts it in *Waiting for Godot*:

Astride of a grave and a difficult birth.
Down in the hole, lingeringly, the gravedigger puts on the
    forceps.
We have time to grow old. The air is full of our cries.
But habit is a great deadener.
At me too someone is looking. Of me too someone is
    saying
He is sleeping, he knows nothing, let him sleep on. (QR51)

I might add here Hamlet's:

I shall win at the odds

My father introduced me to horse racing, and betting on it, when I was eight at the first post-war Derby at Epsom, won by Airborne. He gave me a few pence to back Golden Sorrell in the first race, which won, and he returned my stake and winnings, making me keen on horse racing ever since.

My father recorded all his racing bets so that by the end of his life he could easily prove that he had made a profit, winning at the odds. Mind you, the profit was tiny in relation to the outlay, and if the costs of information and attendances at the tracks were taken into account, he would have paid for his hobby, not won anything from it.

I like the story of a punter having a dreadful day attempting to recoup his losses on the last race of the day betting sufficient funds on two 7/1 shots either to beat the odds-on favourite. The race unfolded happily for him, the two coming well clear in the final furlong, the favourite many lengths behind. As the two battled for the victory one lunged into the other, knocking him over, and was thus disqualified despite passing the winning post alone, the result going to the third horse; the punter had lost at the odds.

And it should be noted, as with the unlucky punter, Hamlet – *I shall win at the odds* – was, in fact, well on his way to winning the wager until he was foully and fatally struck down by Laertes' poisoned foil.

There are others than Shakespeare, Marlowe and Beckett, who are authors of red letter words, who have contributed to my pleasure in language. I have mentioned the *English Sampler* that provided so much of my knowledge, appreciation and admiration of English literature. Many of the quoted examples helped me through my degree, and many have stayed with me throughout my life, several being my show-off quotations. It feels right to record some of these pleasures if only to prompt interest in others who haven't yet encountered them.

I begin with *Sir Gawain and the Green Knight*, a poem we studied at Cambridge, a fantastic tale described as "one of the greatest works of the English Middle Ages and perhaps the greatest triumph of the English alliterative tradition." I have performed a version at Christmas (the significant day of the poem); I found the Green Chapel in the snow near Buxton; I have an illustration by Paul Birkbeck he did for a television version. The loveliness of the lady: *Her brest bare before and behind eke* is a powerful image; the alliterative verse is difficult to understand literally, but not imaginatively through the rhythm. This is an example of its power:

Cloudes casten kenly the colde to the erthe,
With nye innough of the northe the naked to tene;
The snowe sintered ful snart, that snayped the wylde;
The werbelande wynde sapped fro the high
And drof uch dale ful of dry fles ful grete.

My second example is also of Old English which I take from the Wakefield Master's *Second Shepherd's Play* where Mak the sheep stealer invades the mystery of Christ's birth. This version in the Everyman text was one of my first efforts at directing at the Tower Theatre. This time the quotation is of a poor man's tribulations that has a modern ring to it.

One of the shepherds speaks:

But we sely husbands that walk on the moor
In faith, we are near-hands out of the door.
No wonder, as it stands, if we be poor,
For the tilth of our lands lies fallow as the floor,
As ye ken.
We are so hammed,
For taxed and rammed,
We are made hand-tamed
With these gentlery-men

Try reading both of these Old English passages aloud to get the full power of the words.

The English language reached its apogee in the sixteenth and seventeenth centuries and one of its greatest triumphs of literature is William Tyndale's translation of the Bible; much of which was later included in the King James version. The last chapter of Ecclesiastes is pertinent for young and old, as these extracts demonstrate and echo my own thoughts in this book:

Remember now thy Creator in the days of thy youth, while the evil days come not, nor the years draw nigh, when thou shalt say, I have no pleasure in them... Then shall the dust return to the earth as it was: and the spirit shall return unto God who gave it. Vanity of vanities, saith the Preacher, all is vanity. [57]

Tyndale was burned at the stake for the perceived heresy of his translations, a crime of the dominant Church of the time.

Robert Herrick understood the transitory nature of youth:

Gather ye rosebuds while ye may
Old Time is still a-flying. [58]

And I suppose that Old Time is behind this quotation from Herrick that I always quote to any young beauty called Julia:

Whenas in silks my Julia goes,
Then, then, methinks, how sweetly flows
That liquefaction of her clothes. [59]

John Dryden next is memorable for his witty satire of the Duke of Buckingham, whose play, *The Rehearsal*, had caricatured Dryden. This is Dryden's response:

In the first rank of these did Zimri stand:
A man so various that he seemed to be
Not one, but all mankind's epitome.
Stiff in opinions, always in the wrong;
Was everything by starts, and nothing long:
But in the course of one revolving moon,
Was chymist, fiddler, statesman and buffoon...

… In squand'ring wealth was his peculiar art;
Nothing went unrewarded, but desert.
Beggar'd by fools, whom still he found too late:
He had his jest, and they had his estate. (60)

An example of William Congreve's dramatic wit is in *The Way of the World*: Lady Wishfort at her toilette with her maid Foible:

Lady: This wretch has fretted me that I am absolutely decay'd. Look Foible.

Foible: Your Ladyship has frowned a little too rashly indeed madam. There are some cracks discernible in the White Varnish.

Lady: Let me see the Glass. Cracks say'st thou? Why I am arrantly flayed. I look like an old peel'd wall. Thou must repair me Foible, before Sir Rowland comes; or I shall never keep up to my picture.

Alexander Pope is one of my especial favourites that I quote often, a brilliant stylist and shrewd thinker whose influence may have waned in recent years though I am certain will rise again. As a thinker his *Essay on Man* is still highly relevant

Know then thyself, presume not God to scan,
The proper study of mankind is Man.
Plac'd on this isthmus of a middle state,
A being darkly wise and rudely great…
… Created half to rise, and half to fall;
Great lord of all things, yet a prey to all;
Sole judge of truth, in endless error hurl'd;
The glory, jest and riddle of the world!

And from *The Rape of the Lock* I love his technical brilliance in describing the Baron's act of cutting the lock of hair from Belinda's head. In a couplet of two lines Pope describes five distinct motions:

> The peer now spreads (1) The Glitt'ring Forfex wide (2),
> T'inclose the Lock (3), now joins it (4) to divide (5).

It's amazing.

Amazing too was Samuel Johnson's perseverance in completing his *Dictionary of the English Language,* as he wrote to his diffident patron Lord Chesterfield:

> Is not a patron, my Lord, one who looks with
> unconcern on a man struggling for life in the water,
> and, when he has reached ground, encumbers him
> with help? The notice which you had been pleased
> to take of my labours, had it been early, had been
> kind; but it has been delayed till I am indifferent, and
> cannot enjoy it; till I am solitary and cannot impart it;
> till I am known and do not want it.

I made my first purchase of antiquarian books as a student in Cambridge – the collected works of Laurence Sterne. I love *Tristram Shandy* which is full of:

> Digressions, incontestably are the sunshine – they are
> the life, the soul of reading…

And the *Sentimental Journey* has this wonderful ending:

> But the fille de chamber … had crept silently out of
> her closet, and it being totally dark, had stolen so close

to our beds, that she had got herself into the narrow passage which separated them, and had advanced so far up as to be in a line betwixt her mistress and me – so that when I stretched out my hand, I caught hold of the fille de chambre's.

The supreme stylist and historian, Edward Gibbon, puts his huge achievement into a personal context. He records his emotions on completing the *Decline and Fall of the Roman Empire*:

> The air was temperate, the sky was serene, the silver orb of the moon was reflected from the waters, and all nature was silent…
>
> But my pride was soon humbled and sober melancholy was spread over my mind by the idea that I had taken an everlasting leave of an old and agreeable companion, and that, whatsoever might be the future date of my History, the life of the historian must be short and precarious.

Richard Sheridan built on Shakespeare when it came to Malapropisms. Here are two.

> Illiterate him, I say, quite from your memory

> She's as headstrong as an allegory on the banks of the Nile. [61]

Sydney Smith, the wisest of churchmen, was a compassionate tutor of his family and household – witness his pride in the achievements of Bunch, his housemaid turned butler. His recipe for a salad dressing is brilliantly expressed:

Let onion atoms lurk within the bowl
And scarce-suspected, animate the whole [62]

Samuel Taylor Coleridge was the oldest of the so-called Romantic Poets. I love this from *Kubla Khan*

A damsel with a dulcimer
in a vison once I saw:
It was an Abyssinian maid
And on her dulcimer she played
Singing of Mount Abora.

Percy Bysshe Shelley next, and I particularly like his *Ode to the West Wind*, which on writing down I see I have been misquoting, but here it is right:

O Wild West Wind, thou breath of Autumn's being,
Thou, from whose unseen presence the leaves dead
Are driven, like ghosts from an enchanter fleeing,
Yellow, and black, and pale, and hectic red,
Pestilence-stricken multitudes: O thou,
Who chariotest to their dark wintry bed
The winged seeds, where they lie cold and low…

Autumn is also the theme of John Keats's ode and I remember Colonel Hills, my headmaster, performing it for us in Bradfield's Greek Theatre:

Season of mists and mellow fruitfulness,
Close bosom-friend of the maturing sun;
Conspiring with him how to load and bless
With fruit the vines [63]

And, the Colonel went on, from another ode, to the Nightingale:

> O, for a draught of vintage! that hath been
> Cool'd a long age in the deep-delved earth,
> Tasting of Flora and the country green,
> Dance, and Provençal song and sunburnt mirth!
> O for a beaker full of the warm South,
> Full of the true, the blushful Hippocrene,
> With beaded bubbles winking at the brim,
> And purple-stained mouth…

Robert Browning has a special place in my heart; and my performances of *My Last Duchess* and *The Bishop Orders his Tomb* are on record. This is the latter's ending:

> And leave me in my church, the church for peace,
> That I may watch at leisure if he leers –
> Old Gandolf, at me, from his onion-stone,
> As still he envied me, so fair she was! [QR52] [QR53]

Of the Victorians; Oscar Wilde is pre-eminent. I have always loved this:

> It really makes no matter, Algernon. I had some
> crumpets with Lady Harbury, who seems to me to be
> living entirely for pleasure now. [64]

William Butler Yeats was Tom Henn's (my tutor at Cambridge) special favourite and this is too often relevant:

> Turning and turning in the widening gyre,
> The falcon cannot hear the falconer;

Things fall apart; the centre cannot hold;
Mere anarchy is loosed upon the world,
The blood-dimmed tide is loosed, and everywhere
The ceremony of innocence is drowned;
The best lack all conviction, while the worst
Are full of passionate intensity. [65]

My grandfather P.T.R. knew T. S. Eliot, who signed several works for him. Eliot is the modern poet who means much to me. I talk of *Four Quartets* elsewhere, and The *Waste Land* is outstanding. On a personal note that fits the rest of the book, I quote this from *The Love Song of J. Alfred Prufrock:*

No! I am not Prince Hamlet, nor was meant to be;
Am an attendant lord, one that will do
To swell a progress, start a scene or two,
Advise the prince; no doubt, an easy tool,
Deferential, glad to be of use,
Politic, cautious, and meticulous;
Full of high sentence, but a bit obtuse;
At times, indeed, almost ridiculous –
Almost, at times, the Fool.

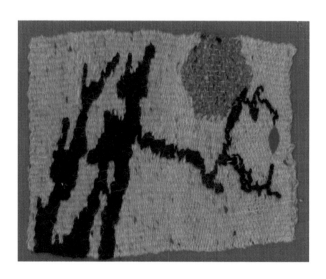

ITERATION IN ART

No Matter; Try Again

Some of the points from the Seven Stars Projects turn up several times in those chapters and sometimes in different chapters and in new guises. I call these iterations in art and this chapter is to describe some of them.

A Tree

The first is a blasted tree in North Weald Park. My mother and I had (unusually) gone for a walk in this park. I was about seventeen and had my first camera, an Ilford, with me. We came upon this tree which was in an advanced state of decay. The trunk was completely split in two giving the impression of two figures, one with a head forked like a beetle, the other with one thin branch held out at right angles, supporting another twin branch reaching vertically. The whole suggested two demented dancers.

Six years later I came to direct *Waiting for Godot*. Beckett's play takes place on a country road by a tree. I asked Frank Corkery to design the set based on my blasted tree – the split trunk neatly suggesting the dualities of the play: Vladimir/Estragon; Pozzo/Lucky; Mind/Body; Master/Slave; Saved Thief/Damned Thief; White Beard/Black Beard; Sheep Minding/Goat Minding; You/Your brother; Speech/Dumbness; Sight/Blindness; Bare/Covered with leaves. Beckett specifically asks for the tree to have a few leaves in the second act, whereas it was bare before. This suggests hope, and it is hopefulness – "Well? Shall we go? Yes, let's go."

[They do not move] – that seems to be the final note of the play. The single leaf on the blasted bough has come to signify hope for me. Sheila later made a small woven tapestry of the tree for a birthday present.

One of my perennial projects has been the play of *Pericles* which is best described in my introduction to the film script of *Fathers and Daughters*. The emblem carried by the shipwrecked and destitute Pericles to a tournament is a withered branch, with a few leaves, his circumstances having left him little time to prepare better for it. Thaisa, whose birthday is to be honoured at the tournament, describes his emblem:

> Thaisa: He seems to be a stranger; but his present is
> A wither'd branch that's only green at top;
> The motto "In hac spe vivo".
>
> Simonides: A pretty moral;
> From the dejected state wherein he is
> He hopes by you his fortunes yet may flourish. [67]

Ronnie Copas included the Godot tree in his painting *The Poet and the Painter*.

When I played Prospero in 2006 I adorned his magic staff with a leaf. For my second production of *Waiting for Godot* I again asked for the same tree to be the main feature of the set. In 2015 I played King Lear, and in the mad scene carried a ragged staff with leaves, the same idea but not in this case signifying hope. I used it as a mock bow to threaten the chasing soldiers on my exit.

A Dancer

The next iteration concerns the Barong Play in Bali that the family attended on a holiday from Malaysia. This is performed every day in a village for what today has become a tourist attraction. It is the local version of the Ramayana and it is performed in an open air courtyard bedecked with greenery and flowers. The origin is religious and is deeply serious. A gamelan troupe provides the musical continuity. There are dances, mimes, colourful costumes and slapstick. One who captivated me entirely was a woman in her early 30s, as I guessed, playing the young prince beset by evils, the leading role in the play. Hers was a world-class performance.

Being in the open air and thus being able to take photographs saw me loose off at least three reels (those were the days of celluloid which came 36 to the cassette, so, about 100 pictures in all). I developed them all, enlarged a few and displayed them in my album – a special theatrical collection. I asked the designer Sue Plummer to rehabilitate an old magnificent Victorian screen which had fallen on hard times. We had bought this from an antique store, decorated with interesting ephemera from the late Victorian period. Many of the fifteen panels (30 in all, the panels being two-sided) had been badly damaged. Sue was asked to rescue as much of the Victoriana as possible, reassembling them on the fifteen panels one side of the screen. The obverse panels now being blank I enlarged fifteen of the Bali photographs which Sue mounted and embellished so that the screen could be opened showing the Bali or the Victorian sides depending on one's mood at the moment. This screen is now with Owen in the USA.

I decided to use my favourite picture of all, that I describe as theatrical ecstasy, of the prince hard up against the bright green shrubbery, her head half enclosed by green, eyes shut, in a pose of high theatrical intensity. I commissioned John Lawson, a senior artist at Goddard and Gibbs, the stained glass company, to make a panel of this picture to celebrate our 25th wedding anniversary. I inscribed it with "O Mistress Mine", the same words as engraved on the inside of Sheila's wedding ring, and added the monogram R$^C_4$S to commemorate the event. And eight and one third years later I commissioned a second variant for our 33⅓ wedding or R$^C_3$S. And I later bought John Lawson's original cartoon which is now adorned with cut out figures from the play.

I sometimes think of revisiting Bali to seek out this lady, who must by now be into her 60s, probably directing performances of the play, or basking in a benign retirement, to show her these iterations of that performance all those years ago. But for whose benefit? And may she not be lonely and forgotten, or dead, for all I know? She does live on in these notes and images, though she is not aware of this particular tribute and applause. Oh well.

It is convenient to mention here two other items of stained glass.

The first, we bought in the Portobello Road, of four figures holding various produce with the quotation

O mickle is the powerful grace that lies
In herbs, plants, stones and their true qualities. [68]

Contemplating the purchase, with my brother John who was visiting from the USA, I recognised this as being from *Pericles* and said so. "Nonsense" said a woman next to me "It's *Romeo and Juliet*." Of course she's right: it's Friar Laurence's first speech which carries on:

For naught so vile that on the earth doth live
But to the earth some special good doth give

This was housed in lavatory glass, as I call it, and the same Goddard and Gibbs firm rehoused it to fit a big window upstairs in our holiday house on the Isle of Dogs. I gave it to John when we sold the house and it now adorns his study in Oceanside.

The second piece features a panel called music, a beautifully painted grave maiden holding a lyre. I guess it had once been part of a Victorian or Edwardian conservatory. This too was given fresh modern surrounding glass by Goddard and Gibbs. Much later I had it mounted in a wooden frame with internal lighting by Simon Kidd and gave it to us for our Golden Wedding i.e. $R^C_2 S$. The figure is St Cecilia representing music, and Sheila is the anglicised version of the Saint's name.

A Nude

Anna was a model at John Monks's life class that Sheila and I attended. She was not only very handsome, but thoroughly professional in all she did. "I know the value of my body, and how to use it" she said. As my efforts at drawing were not very good I decided to ask her if she would be a photographic model. To protect her identity I suggested that we use a mask for her face so as to avoid any "sexy" pouts, as used by *Sun* page 3 models, and to protect her should the pictures ever escape my control, on the Internet, for example, though I assured her they were only for my private collection. That was all agreed and I purchased a wonderful Venetian carnival mask with a gold face topped with cock's feathers, for the purpose.

I decided to show off the stained glass and took pictures of Anna posing by them, often using mirrors to double the effect. The collection both in colour and in black and white pleased me very much, so much so that I have never felt it necessary to do it again with another model. I remember P.T.R.'s many watercolours of the naked female form, a taste which I have inherited with the same passion.

Often I made several multiple montages of the photographs including taking a photocopy of one, not on paper but on a transparency, which served as a cheap bit of "stained glass" on my study window, itself photographed several times subsequently against the trees of the square or in unusual light. And I iterated the image even further by getting Norman at Goddard and Gibbs to create a four-pane montage for a window that overlooked the Thames.

The most ambitious iteration was the mosaic I made of one of the pictures. This had Anna reclining on a chaise longue with a blue patterned drape across her waist and thighs. I attended a mosaic class one year and decided to iterate this image by making the drape appear as a rushing stream making a small waterfall (water). The gold face of the mask was the sun rising through the trees (including a Godot tree) against a blue sky (air). From the ground below the waterfall (earth) rises the smoke of a fire with sparks of red (fire).

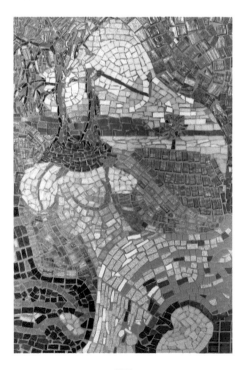

During the shoot Anna removed the mask as if content to proceed freely. Indeed she gave me a wonderful image of the mask, this time placed on the back of her head with the eyeholes showing tresses of hair only, which dropped to her shoulders below the face of the mask. This fills the bottom of a two-image piece of stained glass (again by Goddard and Gibbs) below a splendid portrait of Anna, divested of the mask.

Though not strictly a portrait of Anna, and not a nude, we bought a picture of her by John Monks which featured in the short film the girls and I made of *My Last Duchess* – the picture being:

> That's my last Duchess painted on the wall,
> Looking as if she were alive;
> I call that piece a wonder, now: [69]

It fits the poem brilliantly.

And though not strictly an iteration I mention the board in my bedroom. This was constructed for me by Simon Kidd, to my design, based on the idea in Sir John Soane's Museum where the Hogarths are displayed on moveable frames that allow two displays to appear on one wall. Mine has a central frame which can hold pictures in a way that does not interfere with the six folding panels of four sides each that are hinged to the outside of the frame. When the panels are folded over the frame one sees six pictures commissioned from Dorian Millman: R.P.J. as Cassius at Bradfield; Colley Cibber; Fred Radley as Vladimir; Ecstasy in Bali; Ian McKellen as Dr Faustus for *The Genius of Christopher Marlowe*; and R.P.J. as Prospero in Paris. The other three panels of each set of four can be displayed at will by folding outwards or by folding back over the central frame. Most of these have ephemera but each has a guiding logic. The walls behind the central frame also serve to display pictures and ephemera, the displays changing occasionally as new material comes in or displays are reorganised. The whole has the feel (especially in low light) of a pleasing mosaic of different sized rectangles which give a harmonious impression of (mainly) theatrical memories.

A Stone

The next of the main iterations is the stone I found on Aphrodite's beach in Cyprus when I was researching film locations for *Fathers and Daughters* – my version of *Pericles*. Aphrodite's beach is one of the jewels of the island of Cyprus – where the naked form of the Greek goddess was born from the waves. The place is remarkable for some beautiful offshore rocks and for a beach full of round pebbles. I had not been to Cyprus until well into my sixties (though I had seen it from the air – a vision of a paradise island from the Shackleton aircraft taking me, an air cadet, to Iraq for a short visit). In researching the locations for the film I came to the conclusion that Cyprus with its architectural mixture of classical, crusader, Turkish and Middle Eastern styles would be an appropriate location for a film that is set in Ephesus, Mytilene, Tyre, Tarsus, Pentapolis and Antioch. I had selected Aphrodite's beach for the place where Thaisa's coffin comes ashore near to Cerimon's house. Thaisa, the wife of Pericles, had been in a storm at sea where, at the height of the storm, her daughter *Call'd Marina for I was born at sea* had been born. Thaisa had died in childbirth and, since the storm showed no sign of abating, and according to the sailors' superstition would not abate until the dead was consigned to the deep, it was her coffin that eventually would end up on the shores of Ephesus, near Cerimon's house.

Cerimon is a doctor and, on opening the coffin, perceives that Thaisa is not dead and may recover, and she does in fact do so, remembering that she had been in labour, but unaware of whether she had given birth or not. My notion, at this point, was to have included in the coffin (along with the other evidence that had been put there to identify the corpse) a stone, the stone that I had found on the beach. The stone is of a size and smoothness that suggests a baby's head – a powerful metaphor of the apparent barrenness of Thaisa's childbirth. In the final scene she is reunited with Marina, and the stone that Thaisa had always kept with her in memory of the barren childbirth is replaced in her grasp by the head of her new found daughter Marina.

When it finally became evident that the film would not be made in Cyprus I kept the stone and brought it to England as an image that might iterate.

In discussing the leaf (with its *Pericles* connection) I mentioned the leaf atop Prospero's staff. A leaf adorns the stone. The stone itself, unadorned, also played its part in *The Tempest* – first as a planetary symbol that Prospero used to invoke the tempest. Later, in the great soliloquy.

Ye elves of hills, brooks, standing lakes, and groves;

It became the visual emblem in turn of the moon, the sun and the earth, all referred to in the speech. And, in its latest iteration the stone sits on my desk, with a bay leaf from Sheila's garden attached atop.

I must also mention that passage in Beckett's *Molloy* They were pebbles but I call them stones, in which Molloy sets himself the task of circulating (say) sixteen stones around the pockets of his trousers and greatcoat, sucking them turn and turnabout so that each of the sixteen is sucked in impeccable succession, once and once only until the sequence is to be repeated. I first saw this performed in New York in one of his last performances, by Jack MacGowran in the *Works of Beckett* in a programme endorsed by Beckett himself. I still have, and treasure, to the extent of having had it stabilised and preserved, a fly leaf advertising this show – MacGowran's ravaged face the impelling image; and subsequently I chose to perform what is a 15-minute monologue at various dinner parties to guests and friends. And when I decided at 69 to record *Krapp's Last Tape* for posterity I asked Michael Burrell to do this piece at the same time. We filmed *Stones* on the south coast with Burrell reading to his pre-recorded voice of the monologue, except the first lines which he spoke:

> I took advantage of being at the seaside to lay in a store of sucking stones. They were pebbles but I call them stones.

And the last:

> And the solution to which I rallied in the end was to throw away all the stones but one, which I kept now in one pocket, now in another, and which of course I soon lost, or threw away, or gave away, or swallowed.

I did subsequently perform *Stones* on film for myself, and this version is available on the website. (QR54)

A Mask

The terracotta Greek mask of tragedy is the first souvenir I ever bought during the trip to Greece in that summer vacation of 1960 that I undertook with Douglas Adler, with whom I have remained friends since 1950. I first met him at the scholarship entrance exam for Bradfield. We were both in the Greek play of our year which was *Oedipus at Colonus*, and the play subsequently visited Saarbrucken to take part in a Delphiade of various Greek plays performed by a wide range of European universities (and Bradfield). I was cast as Antigone and Douglas was in the chorus.

One of Antigone's speeches in the play I retained – not being a classical scholar I had simply learned it by rote, imitating Raeburn who preferred to have good actors he could impart Greek to, rather than Greek scholars who may or may not have been able to act. These few lines of intense desolation (A "threnody" one critic called it) have stood me in good stead namely:

To clinch my place at St Catharine's College Cambridge when the senior tutor, Tom Henn, was inclined to admit students (even to give them exhibitions) who could act.

In various Greek and Roman theatres, as a show-off tourist playing to Sheila and various co-travellers.

In Indonesia, having performed a bit of Shakespeare to respond to my host's jocular observation: I suppose you could do Sophocles as well – "Only in Greek" I said.

In Cyprus to Andy Bargilly and others involved in the theatre there, whose aid I was seeking for *Fathers and Daughters* – whose observation after I finished of a performance that had obviously had little resonance for them gallantly opined "Ah yes; the Erasmus Pronunciation."

The theatre at Bradfield was modelled on Epidaurus it is said, though Epidaurus is huge in comparison. We visited Epidaurus in 1960 where we saw the only performance (of six or so advertised) of Maria Callas in Bellini's *Norma*, seen from Row 55 (that's far back) where the features of the singers could not be identified but where the voices were perfectly heard – an amazing experience, one of those that one can bore one's friends with, saying "I was there." During my visits to Cyprus I also visited Epidaurus when the Cyprus National Theatre were performing *Seven Against Thebes*.

The mask of this section could have been copied from an ancient mask from the theatre at Delphi. And, though not strictly an iteration it is suitable here to iterate my experiences of Delphi, amid the olive groves, where three roads meet.

We travelled to Greece in 1960 as students from university and we spent about three weeks travelling around, often by train, visiting all the notable sites. It so happened we were in Patras and rather than visit Delphi via Athens we took a boat across the Gulf of Corinth to Itea, a small port on the opposite side. We took a taxi to Delphi up the mountain covered with olive trees. The taxi driver, hearing our language, insisted that we paid nothing, remembering what the British had done for Greece in the war.

As with most of the places we visited we hardly knew what to expect, such was our general ignorance of anything but the name of each place, but this gave us a huge benefit in that we could discover each place as if we were the first explorers. Delphi was a notable example of this and, it being early in the morning there, after our taxi ride, we were alone in our discovery.

First the temple of Apollo on a small promontory overlooking the valley of olives. Then the Pierian spring

> A little learning is a dangerous thing;
> Drink deep, or taste not the Pierian spring: [70]

Moving up the mountain we saw the Treasury first, and then the site of the Oracle which Leontes so categorically denigrated

> There is no truth at all i' the Oracle [71]

though, in his defence, the Oracle was always equivocal in its pronouncements.

We continued upwards and came to the theatre with a stunning view of the olive groves in the valley. Knowing something of

Greek theatre I had insisted that we booked for a performance of *Oedipus Tyrannus* at the Herod Atticus theatre later in our visit, on account of the legendary great actor Alexis Minotis who, with his wife, Katina Paxinou, had restored the ancient texts to prominence after the war. It was said that Minotis when performing the play at Delphi had timed the opening of the play so that, when he re-enters after the blinding, blood streaming down his face, the olive groves turned red in the sunset – which was known to happen every evening at an easily predicted time.

The only disappointment of our trip was that the performance in Athens was cancelled and I never saw Minotis or Paxinou, though we did see a production of *Iphigenia in Aulis* about which I can recall nothing.

Delphi was not finished for us since we climbed further to the ancient stadium in a remarkable state of preservation, a complete surprise to us who had assumed that Olympia was the one and only site of athletic games. And, sitting on the arena seats, staring up into the sky we saw eagles circling around the summit of Mount Olympus.

After this it is not surprising that Delphi continued to be of seminal importance in my life.

Sheila and I visited Delphi on our honeymoon a few years later in 1964, and we returned to Greece only in December 2004 to celebrate three anniversaries: our ruby wedding, Sheila's 65th birthday and my 66⅔ birthday. Our ruby wedding had been celebrated on October 3rd 2004, Sheila's birthday on December 5th (while we were in Athens) and my significant birthday on December 8th which I planned to celebrate in Delphi. We duly set out on the 7th and arrived to settle in our hotel to allow me to visit the Oracle the following morning.

As in my student days, I arrived at the deserted site in the early morning leaving Sheila asleep. And, as I had tentatively planned,

I sought to consult the Oracle, but not necessarily the Oracle of Apollo. I walked up to the theatre and, standing in the orchestra looking up at the deserted seats I asked "Am I an actor about to perform in front of an empty house?" I then moved up to the auditorium and, looking down to the stage, I asked "Am I an auditor for a play that will not take place?"

At that moment, across the valley, I heard the tinkle of a sheep's bell and a flock of sheep went by, with a shepherd driving them. Surely that was the Oracle speaking, or at least the Oracle of theatre. For I had just finished playing the shepherd in *Oedipus Tyrannus*, which is set in Delphi. The shepherd had looked after the young Oedipus abandoned by his parents, who had been told that Oedipus would one day kill his father and marry his mother. Here I was an actor, occupying a middle ground between professionalism and non-professionalism – I had played the shepherd in a professional production though I had agreed to do it for no fee.

My questions in Delphi's theatre were possibly being answered. And remembering that the Oracle can be equivocal, is always equivocal, its answers could have been: Yes, that I was destined not to appear before an audience, or even (like not seeing Minotis in Athens) destined to be denied a wished-for event; or No, that the reverse may turn out to be true. Or that one answer might be No and the other Yes, or contrariwise. I decided not to trust the Oracle, and trust it completely, and carry on.

A few years later, in Toledo, I came across a mosaic in a museum, unequivocally of a shepherd (with his crook) wearing a Greek tragic mask just like my tourist souvenir of my student visit. I mused that the number of actors who have played this part since the mosaic was made is small. I am one of them and still have the mask. And I persevered with my theatrical career, despite, or perhaps as answered by, the Oracle.

The weather vane is my last example of iteration in art. It sits on top of a house overlooking the Thames. It is the tree that suggested the sets for *Waiting for Godot* and Sheila's tapestry, and is adorned with the leaf of hope which features on the stone and in Pericles's emblem. Hope is what I feel at the end of *Waiting for Godot* where Vladimir and Estragon agree to depart, but are followed by the stage direction

(They do not move)

The house, incidentally, is Ian McKellen's, who played Estragon in a world tour of the play, despite my advising him to play Vladimir when he asked my opinion as to which of the two he should play. How right he was in the event.

You may recall that this chapter started with the Godot tree and this iteration ends with the same image.

AFTERWORD

I do not believe in the afterlife for two reasons: first, what is in it for God? And second, as suggested by Sir Tom Stoppard,

"Eternity, where will it end?"

Nearing my own end, my own afterlife will be in the memories of those that knew me, and in my books and diaries, if there are any interested readers in later years.

The Foreword opened with words from *Hamlet*.

I conclude this Afterword with words from *Troilus and Cressida*, which I have already quoted, and which remain for me the most valuable and consoling words as I contemplate the afterlife. Or not.

> O, let not virtue seek
> Remuneration for the thing it was;
> For beauty, wit,
> High birth, vigour of bone, desert in service,
> Love, friendship, charity, are subjects all
> To envious and calumniating time. (QR52)

I am happy with that.

Acknowledgements

I am indebted to many colleagues for the preparation of *Red Letter Words*. My thanks and gratitude to:

Sam and Alice Carter of Tandem Publishing

John Wheeler of Copyprints

Lily and Alana McGeough of Lilana Films

Sharon Clay for many versions of the typescript

David Simon, ex-Chief Executive Officer of BP plc

And to the artists who provided such wonderful illustrations:

Paul Birkbeck	Bill Dudley
Ronnie Copas	Clive Francis

All of whom became personal friends while contributing their artistry.

To Artistic Directors of the Tower Theatre and Directors of individual productions:

John Barton	Nigel Martin	Martin South
Roger Beaumont	John Morton	Ruth Sullivan
Michael Burrell	Martin Mulgrew	Brian Tapply
Robert Gillespie	David Raeburn	Penny Tuerk
James Horne	Sara Randall	Dennis Turner
Clyde Jones	Corin Redgrave	Trevor Williams
Colin Ley	Ralph Shafran	Margery Withers

I must pay a special acknowledgment to the founders of the Tower Theatre, Frank and Molly Smith, and to Laurence Tuerk and Stephen Ley, who supported me in all my major projects so brilliantly.

To acting colleagues:

Peta Barker	Allan Hart	Richard Pederson
Dominic Batty	Ian Hoare	Fred Radley
Jill Batty	Walter Kennedy	Ian Recordon
John Chapman	Alison Linney	David Rowe-Beddoe
Annie Connell	John McEnery	Jill Ruane
David Coombs	Denise McPherson	Paul Rutledge
Edgar Davies	John McSpadyen	Ella Slack
Suzanne Doggett	Terry Marlowe	Ruth Sullivan
Bill Dudley	Jules Melvin	Valerie Testa
Richard Earthy	Derek Mudie	Tom Tillery
Haidee Elise	Jonathan Norris	Valerie Whitehouse
Patanne Fairfoot	Peter Novis	Pam Withers
Philip Fasham	Bobbie Peacock	

To technical and supporting members of the Tower Theatre:

Sarah Ambrose	John Dorsett	Dinah Irvine
Stephen Brasher	Bill Dudley	Ruth Norris
Sheila Burbidge	Colin Guthrie	Sue Plummer
Jean Carr	Peter Hebbes	David Taylor
Jude Chalk	Nick Inslie	Peter Westbury
Richard Davies	Roanne Inslie	

And the photographers of the productions, including Ruth Anthony, Bryan Bane and David Sprecher. For the photograph of the Little Gidding tree, Paul Skirrow.

Red Letter References

References not identified in the text.

WS: William Shakespeare   SB: Samuel Beckett
CM: Christopher Marlowe   GOC: Gentleman of Cambridge

Red Letter Number	Page	Reference
1	ix	SB *Waiting for Godot*
2	ix	WS *Troilus and Cressida*
3	1	Ecclesiastes XII
4	2	John Osborne *The Entertainer*
5	3	SB *Krapp's Last Tape*
6	3	Alexander Pope *The Temple of Fame*
7	4	Thomas Gray *Elegy Written in a Country Churchyard*
8	4	CM *The Jew of Malta*
9	6	Brian Friel *Translations*
10	10	WS *Two Gentlemen of Verona*
11	11	James Shirley 'The Contention of Ajax and Ulysses'
12	11	WS *King Henry V*
13	15	William Wycherley *The Country Wife*
14	19	WS *Othello*
15	19	WS *Othello*
16	19	WS *Troilus and Cressida*
17	20	WS *Antony and Cleopatra*
18	28	WS *Troilus and Cressida*
19	30	WS *Coriolanus*

20	38	WS *King Henry VI Part II*
21	41	WS *As You Like It*
22	50	Brian Friel *Translations*
23	61	WS *King Lear*
24	72	SB *All That Fall*
25	72	SB *Krapp's Last Tape*
26	75	SB *Waiting for Godot*
27	77	SB *Krapp's Last Tape*
28	78	SB *Endgame*
29	79	SB *Endgame*
30	79	SB *Happy Days*
31	80	SB *All That Fall*
32	81	Tom Stoppard *Rosencrantz and Guildenstern are Dead*
33	84	WS *King Lear*
34	88	WS *Timon of Athens*
35	105	WS *The Winter's Tale*
36	106	WS *The Winter's Tale*
37	107	WS *A Midsummer Night's Dream*
38	108	WS *King Richard II*
39	108	WS *Macbeth*
40	108	WS *The Tempest*
41	108	WS *Hamlet*
42	108	Ben Jonson from First Folio of WS (1623)
43	112	CM *Dr Faustus*
44	113	WS *King Henry VI Part III*
45	114	CM *Tamburlaine the Great Part II*

46	116	CM *Tamburlaine the Great Part II*
47	127	GOC *The Lady's Preceptor*
48	129	GOC *The Lady's Preceptor*
49	148	GOC *The Lady's Preceptor*
50	155	SB *Waiting for Godot*
51	167	CM *The Jew of Malta*
52	168	SB *Lessness*
53	168	CM *Tamburlaine the Great Part II*
54	170	WS *Troilus and Cressida*
55	170	WS *Hamlet*
56	171	WS *King Henry IV Part II*
57	174	Ecclesiastes XI
58	174	Robert Herrick to Virgins – to make much of time
59	174	Robert Herrick *Upon Julia's Clothes*
60	174	John Dryden *Absalom and Achitophel*
61	177	Richard Sheridan *The Rivals*
62	177	Sydney Smith 'Recipe for salad'
63	178	John Keats *To Autumn*
64	179	Oscar Wilde *The Importance of Being Earnest*
65	180	W. B. Yeats *The Second Coming*
66	183	SB *Waiting for Godot*
67	184	WS *Pericles*
68	187	WS *Romeo and Juliet*
69	191	Robert Browning *My Last Duchess*
70	197	Alexander Pope 'An Essay on Criticism'
71	197	WS *The Winter's Tale*

QR Codes — see https://www.redletterwords.co.uk/

QR REF.	P.	TEXT REF.	MINS	VIA	
1	42	Excerpt of Doll Tearsheet scene in *Henry IV Part II*	4:48	**V** via YouTube	
2	62	From Brian Friel's play *Translations*	5:28	**A** via RLW website	
3	63	From Beckett's play *Endgame*	1:35	**A** via RLW website	
4	88	From Beckett's novel *Molloy* (Stones)	19:56	**V** via YouTube	
5-41	101–106	Notes on illustrations in *The Poet and the Painter*	Under 2	**N** via RLW website	

42	128	From Marlowe's *Tamburlaine the Great Part II*	1	**A** via RLW website	
43	142	From *The Lady's Preceptor* on Love	9:25	**A** via RLW website	
44	160	From *The Lady's Preceptor* on Love		**A** via RLW website	
45	161	From *The Lady's Preceptor* on Gaming		**A** via RLW website	
46	161	From *The Lady's Preceptor* on Books		**A** via RLW website	

47	169	Gower's speech in *Pericles*	1:57	**A** with pictures via RLW website	
48	176	Opening of T. S. Eliot's *Burnt Norton* (4 voices)	0:48	**A** via RLW website	
49	176	Closing of T. S. Eliot's *Little Gidding* (4 voices)	1:02	**A** via RLW website	
50	180	From Marlowe's *Tamburlaine the Great Part II*	1	**A** via RLW website	
51	183	From Beckett's *Waiting for Godot*	6:22	**A** via RLW website	
52	191	From Robert Browning's 'My Last Duchess'	5:53	**V** via YouTube	

53	191	From Robert Browning's *The Bishop Orders His Tomb*	18:30	**V** via YouTube	
54	207	From Beckett's novel *Molloy* (*Stones*)	19:57	**V** via YouTube	
55	215	From *Troilus and Cressida*	1:49	**A** via RLW website